ADVANCED NEGOTIATION TECHNIQUES

Alan McCarthy
Steve Hay

Apress®

Advanced Negotiation Techniques

ISBN-13 (pbk): 978-1-4842-0851-9

ISBN-13 (electronic): 978-1-4842-0850-2

Managing Director: Welmoed Spahr
Acquisitions Editor: Robert Hutchinson
Developmental Editor: Douglas Pundick
Editorial Board: Steve Anglin, Mark Beckner, Gary Cornell, Louise Corrigan, James DeWolf,
    Jonathan Gennick, Robert Hutchinson, Michelle Lowman, James Markham,
    Matthew Moodie, Jeff Olson, Jeffrey Pepper, Douglas Pundick, Ben Renow-Clarke,
    Gwenan Spearing, Matt Wade, Steve Weiss
Coordinating Editor: Rita Fernando
Copy Editor: Kim Wimpsett
Compositor: SPi Global
Indexer: SPi Global
Cover Designer: Friedhelm Steinen-Broo

Distributed to the book trade worldwide by Springer Science+Business Media New York, 233 Spring Street, 6th Floor, New York, NY 10013. Phone 1-800-SPRINGER, fax (201) 348-4505, e-mail orders-ny@springer-sbm.com, or visit www.springeronline.com. Apress Media, LLC is a California LLC and the sole member (owner) is Springer Science + Business Media Finance Inc (SSBM Finance Inc). SSBM Finance Inc is a Delaware corporation.

For information on translations, please e-mail rights@apress.com, or visit www.apress.com.

Apress and friends of ED books may be purchased in bulk for academic, corporate, or promotional use. eBook versions and licenses are also available for most titles. For more information, reference our Special Bulk Sales–eBook Licensing web page at www.apress.com/bulk-sales.

Any source code or other supplementary materials referenced by the author in this text is available to readers at www.apress.com. For detailed information about how to locate your book's source code, go to www.apress.com/source-code/.

Apress Business: The Unbiased Source of Business Information

Apress business books provide essential information and practical advice, each written for practitioners by recognized experts. Busy managers and professionals in all areas of the business world—and at all levels of technical sophistication—look to our books for the actionable ideas and tools they need to solve problems, update and enhance their professional skills, make their work lives easier, and capitalize on opportunity.

Whatever the topic on the business spectrum—entrepreneurship, finance, sales, marketing, management, regulation, information technology, among others—Apress has been praised for providing the objective information and unbiased advice you need to excel in your daily work life. Our authors have no axes to grind; they understand they have one job only—to deliver up-to-date, accurate information simply, concisely, and with deep insight that addresses the real needs of our readers.

It is increasingly hard to find information—whether in the news media, on the Internet, and now all too often in books—that is even-handed and has your best interests at heart. We therefore hope that you enjoy this book, which has been carefully crafted to meet our standards of quality and unbiased coverage.

We are always interested in your feedback or ideas for new titles. Perhaps you'd even like to write a book yourself. Whatever the case, reach out to us at editorial@apress.com and an editor will respond swiftly. Incidentally, at the back of this book, you will find a list of useful related titles. Please visit us at www.apress.com to sign up for newsletters and discounts on future purchases.

The Apress Business Team

Contents

About the Authors

Alan McCarthy has personally conducted high-profile negotiations and also coached other professionals in negotiation throughout his career. He began as an award-winning salesman and negotiated at different times for Rank Xerox, Exxon, Dun and Bradstreet, US Lines, and ICL. In a career spanning more than 30 years, Alan has managed sales teams and personally sold into the financial services, logistics, automotive, information technology, and consultancy sectors.

Alan founded the Resource Development Centre Ltd (RDC) in 1987 and began training, developing, and consulting in negotiating, relationship selling, target account management, and sales team direction. For the past 15 years Alan has focused on training, developing, and coaching experienced negotiators and their executives. He has conducted more than 530 assignments in 40 countries plus 26 of the American states.

Alan's unique style and experiences in high-stake negotiations has resulted in his clients securing "win-win" results in sales, key purchases, and other types of deals. He continues to deliver successful programs to a wide variety of clients including Microsoft, Oracle, BT, and Siemens, plus a large number of smaller companies in a variety of industries. A few clients have used his techniques outside the business environment altogether—in many public-sector organizations and in such areas as international diplomatic services.

Steve Hay has been an associate of RDC since 1987. He began his career as a commercially oriented accountant and then developed a proven record of success in risk management and across a variety of projects and roles in banking, governance, audit, and supply chain management.

Steve has been successful in both the private and public sectors. His consultancy work in the United Kingdom and overseas has benefitted from his track record of driving value creation through continuous improvement and change management—dealing with negotiation, outsourcing, cultural leadership, development and motivation of teams, and helping many senior managers to build successful careers.

The authors' joint projects have mainly been in the following areas:

- Negotiation techniques
- Finance for nonfinancial managers
- Target account planning
- Proposal writing
- Sales management audits

These projects have included negotiation workshops for sellers and for buyers of specialized services such as information technology. We have provided training and development for sales managers, improving their skills and self-confidence in finance and increasing their success in selling to people from a financial background. Our techniques for target account planning have enabled account managers to plan and then execute their strategies for winning more profitable sales of every type and across all sectors of the economy. We have also provided specialist advice and development for sales executives in proposal writing, resulting in increased sales by building and communicating compelling business cases and presenting their real benefits to clients. Our consultancy projects have included overall reviews of sales organizations, using our Sales Audit Blueprint to verify and provide reassurance of best practice and to highlight areas for improvement, helping to deliver change that assures success in meeting sales targets.

Introduction

Welcome to our book on negotiation. For 25 years across 40 countries plus 26 of the American states, the Resource Development Centre Ltd (RDC) has been helping thousands of people conduct successful negotiations of every type. Many of our clients have been businesses striving to sell more successfully. Other clients have improved their buying skills. A few clients have used our techniques outside the business environment altogether—in many public-sector organizations and in such areas as international diplomatic services.

All have benefitted from our approach to negotiation, which is best summarized by the phrase "win-win." The first "win" refers to our own side of the negotiation and indicates that we feel the result is a win for us. The second "win" indicates that the other party to the negotiation also feels that the result is a win for them. This approach aims to ensure that all parties to the negotiation realize they have achieved the best possible results. It isn't about one party winning and the other losing. A satisfactory outcome leaves both parties feeling that they haven't compromised too much, felt threatened or unnecessarily pressurized, or made sacrifices that they didn't want to. This shared win is an important motivator for both parties to be committed to the implementation of the agreement. The RDC philosophy is centered on business ethics and a principled approach to negotiation that seeks to maximize the value of the outcomes for both parties.

Commercial Negotiation

In today's competitive business environment, the absence of effective negotiation is often the single largest contributor to the lack of success. The changing nature and complexity of the relationships between buyers and suppliers in the increasingly challenging and global marketplace means that many business people now need to be collaborative, sophisticated negotiators. To be a great negotiator is to have discipline, creativity, and courage. In working with our clients we have found that ineffective negotiation can arise mainly from the following three basic issues. Often there is a reluctance to engage in negotiation at all. Sometimes there is a simple lack of professional negotiation skills. Finally, the organization may have no adequate framework to plan, guide, and support successful negotiations. This is a pity because, in most commercial situations we have experienced, by the time buyers enter into a negotiation they are probably going to buy and simply want to get the best package possible from the supplier.

Over the last couple of decades we have noticed some interesting changes in the approach that business people are taking to negotiation. Where it was once often seen as a potential threat to be avoided wherever possible, many businesses are now embracing negotiation as just one of many essential skills to wield in the modern commercial world. We are also seeing some polarization: at one end of the spectrum, some organizations are treating more of their requirements as commodities and using a simplified purchasing model. At the opposite end of the spectrum, many organizations are embracing strategic partnerships and expecting negotiations to carry more value, complexity, and risk. Since 2008 we have also seen a rise in the number of organizations using professional negotiators to help them combat the effects of increasing competition. Many buyers are receiving better training in negotiation and are developing and extending their skills into comprehensive supply chain management. People now expect to negotiate, and they see the process as helping to build positive relationships. Principled negotiation can achieve a solution that is acceptable to all parties involved. Most importantly, this pragmatic and cooperative approach encourages repeat business, to the benefit of both parties.

We have also seen an increase in what could be called *cross-cultural* negotiation. Our clients often want to leverage new technology wherever it emerges and seek new markets no matter where they are located. As our clients increasingly acquire resources and services from the global market and sell to other businesses across the world, there is a need for a negotiation model that can bridge those diverse cultures. Most of this book has been written as culturally neutral as possible, and our negotiation techniques are applicable across a wide range of locations, but we have included some specific considerations for negotiating with people from cultures and traditions you may not have dealt with before.

Other Types of Negotiation

Good negotiation skills are not just an asset for the traditional relationship between a seller and a buyer. Sometimes, the most difficult negotiations can be with colleagues in your own organization. Perhaps you need expert advice or to have key resources assigned to help you but find yourself struggling to get priority or to influence people over whom you have no direct authority.

That can be challenging because you want to maintain a good relationship for the next time you need their help. In all areas of life, with colleagues, employers, or even your own family, being able to negotiate well allows you to get what you want without damaging your relationships.

Later in this book we will explore some of the surprising similarities and productive differences between commercial negotiation, diplomatic negotiation, and hostage negotiation. The latter is not just about one person holding a gun to another in a bank. Consider the situation in the middle of tribal negotiations over access to safe artesian water when suddenly armed protagonists seize the only well for miles around while a woman and child are there. A different type of scenario may be kidnap for money, where the analogy to commercial negotiation may be strongest. Consider also what may happen when a retail food company is taken hostage by people contaminating products in its store. Think of the reputation of a celebrity being taken hostage by media phone-hacking. There are some interesting differences of perspective and emphasis that can provide mutual lessons to be learned in commercial, diplomatic, and hostage negotiations as well as in special situations such as a political party seeking to implement its legislative program or lawyers negotiating over litigation and compensation. We will expand on this in several examples covered in later chapters. You will see that much of this book has been informed by all types of negotiations and, in turn, is applicable to these different realms. A lack of ability in negotiation can be the single largest contributor to preventing people and businesses from getting what they want—and what they need.

Our Philosophy of Negotiation

In this book, we'll define negotiation and explain our four "mantras" of negotiation philosophy. We'll work through the five crucial phases of every professional negotiation and what we call the ten golden rules. We'll suggest a ten-point planning process to help you prepare correctly for a successful negotiation. We'll show you how to put together a better "jellyfish"—a way to create more effective proposals during your negotiations. All this will be described in the context of how your organization can ensure success in its deals by creating the appropriate strategies and framework of processes to plan, guide, and support successful negotiations. Finally, we'll emphasize the importance of reflective practice, coaching, and support for people engaged in negotiations. It doesn't matter which side of the negotiating table you are on, this book will help you to achieve your objectives.

A Definition of Negotiation

Our starting point is to clarify why it is that people need to negotiate at all. The main theme of this book is to show you how you should negotiate and to provide key guidelines or rules, but we'll begin in this chapter by explaining why we negotiate in the first place. A good place to start is in the commercial world. Here, we can define *negotiation* as the voluntary and systematic exploration of both parties' interests, with the objective of agreeing on a mutually acceptable compromise that resolves the conflict. Figure 1-1 breaks down this definition into a few key components so that we can talk about each part in detail.

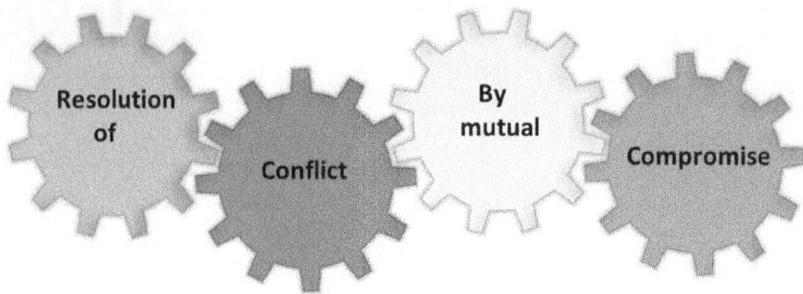

Figure 1-1. A definition of negotiation

We'll touch on hostage negotiation and diplomatic negotiation later in the book, so for now, *conflict* in this context means commercial conflict. Perhaps the most obvious example is when a buyer tells a salesperson that their product is too expensive or they don't want it this week or they don't want it in green. That's what we mean by conflict in the business world.

By *resolution* we mean that by the end of the negotiation we have achieved a satisfactory outcome on our part. But we also mean that the other party also feels that they have obtained a satisfactory outcome. Both parties can see the resolution as a "win-win."

When this fails to happen, it is often because the negotiators forget that part of the definition of negotiation is compromise. You will see later in this book that the first golden rule of negotiation is as follows: don't negotiate unless you need to. If you are a seller, you should sell well and avoid negotiating wherever possible. If you are a buyer, you should buy hard. If this fails and you need to negotiate, then you will have to make some sort of compromise—and so will the other party. That's what's meant by *mutual compromise*. So, before you unintentionally slip into negotiation mode, remember that if you have a superior bargaining position or the other party simply gives you everything you want, then you should promptly close the transaction. You still have the option to negotiate with the other party at some later time, if business circumstances change. Meanwhile, in the more usual situation where the other party puts up an understandable and reasonable resistance to certain elements, you should search for favorable common ground.

Of course, in today's tough economic environment, many businesses are seeing their margins squeezed, and some feel the need to use "gamesmanship" to try to gain an advantage in negotiation. We don't believe the analogy of a game is useful because that suggests negotiation is a sporting talent where luck and finesse are more important than good planning, critical analysis, and sheer hard work. Nevertheless, the other party may be tempted to employ tricks and manipulation. This book will cover such tactics, not least because being forewarned of these techniques is to be forearmed to protect against their use. However, the use of even legitimate gamesmanship runs the risk of the other party feeling they have suffered a loss, which may encourage later reprisals or simply lose you the possibility of a profitable future relationship. This is why we emphasize mutual compromise.

If mutual compromise is not attainable, you may need to simply walk away from the situation. You don't always need to agree on a deal in every attempted commercial negotiation or diplomatic negotiation. That's one of the big differences when it comes to hostage negotiation—where there are unacceptable consequences of failing to agree on a resolution. In the commercial and diplomatic realms, sometimes a poor resolution of conflict is worse than none at all.

The essence of negotiation is compromise, so before you begin any negotiation, you should ask yourself and any other people in your corner if you are all ready, willing, and able to compromise. If you don't really want to negotiate and you don't want to compromise, then don't do it. If you don't know what the negotiation compromise should be or what the cost to you may be, then don't do it. Perhaps the culture of your organization does not encourage true negotiation. Or maybe your part of the organization lacks the capacity to negotiate because you do not have sufficient authority or the mandate to agree on the necessary compromise. If you are in a sales organization, are you ready to drop your price? Are you willing to extend the delivery date? Are you able to change the color of your product? If you are not ready, willing, and able to compromise, then by definition you won't be negotiating.

Similarly, if the other party doesn't recognize the conflict, does not need a resolution, or does not have the ability and desire to compromise, then there will be no mutuality involved. If there is no mutuality, there is no negotiation. In some circumstances, our clients often say they feel the need to aim for a "win-lose," such as when they know they will never again deal with the other party. We have found that in analyzing those circumstances the situation has often not actually been a negotiation as we would define it. Usually, these situations have been good examples of our clients selling well or buying hard and taking a robust commercial approach that proved appropriate and valid. However, caution is recommended. If the other party feels they have suffered a "lose" and still have to deliver some aspect of the deal, they may see the chance for reprisals against you.

A Little Bit of Theory

This chapter is crafted from a practical perspective, based on hard-won experience over a quarter of a century. However, it is useful just to clarify key terms by referring quickly to one aspect of the theory of negotiation. In particular, to explain our overall approach and philosophy, it is useful to distinguish between what can be called *distributive* and *integrative* negotiation. Distributive bargainers think of negotiation as a process of distributing a fixed amount of value. Their objective is to grab as much as possible of the pot before somebody else beats them to it. This approach is often called "win-lose" because it assumes that one person's gain is at the expense of another person's loss.

This is similar to the difficulty that new students of economics often have when first studying the subject. If the world's total economy is valued at a certain sum, how is it possible to grow the overall economy? Surely the only question is how the total pot can be distributed in different ways among all the countries and people on Earth—and isn't that where exploitation rears its ugly head? However, one of the defining characteristics of humanity over the ages has been our ability to excel at certain skills and to specialize in them, leaving other people to excel at their own skills. Such specialization enables one group of people to become efficient at a particular set of tasks while another group becomes efficient at a different set of tasks.

Another defining characteristic of humanity has been our relentless drive to trade with other people. One isolated group could try to prospect for all the natural resources they need, producing every single tool they require and hunting or gathering their own food. However, the willingness and ability to trade opens the door to a different way of life. It becomes possible for people to focus on the things they can do more efficiently than others and then trade their surplus for the things they need that others can produce more efficiently. Specialization combined with trading can create the conditions necessary for a virtuous spiral that grows the overall economy. Total economic value is no longer fixed; the pot can expand.

When we apply that economic model to negotiation, we embrace the concept called *integrative* negotiation. The idea is to build trust so that the parties can be honest about their underlying interests and seek a "win-win" resolution. Rather than locking the parties into a set of confrontational stances, this principled approach to negotiation avoids a personalized joust. It seeks a fair deal for both parties, but one that they can both be motivated toward because it maximizes their own payoff. Later in the book we'll explain how this approach can be extended to create additional value above and beyond the value that either of the parties involved in the negotiation could find in isolation. At first, this may sound a bit like the magic of alchemy, which believes that base metals may be transmuted into gold. But there may be a serious lesson to be learned from alchemy, which coins the Latin maxim *solve et coagula*, meaning to separate and to join together. This resonates with our approach to negotiation, where we first separate fact from perception and emotion from pragmatism before joining the parties together in understanding and cooperation, resulting in the creation of more value.

To summarize, for the purpose of this chapter we are defining negotiation as the voluntary and systematic exploration of both parties' interests with the objective of agreeing on a mutually acceptable compromise that resolves their conflict.

Strategies for Resolving Conflict

Of course, negotiation isn't the only way to resolve conflict. There are five options that we can use to resolve conflict, as follows:

- Negotiation
- Dictating terms
- Surrendering
- Arbitration
- Problem solving

At the top of the list is *negotiation*—where we aim for a "win-win" mutual compromise. The second option is to dictate terms. Here we could state our position as "There's our price; take it or leave it." *Terms* could be dictated by the parties on either side of the table, whether they're buying or selling. A buyer might say, "This is the price I want to pay; take it or leave it. If you don't accept it, I'll go somewhere else." This approach has no element of compromise, and there is no mutuality, so by definition this is not a negotiation.

If you are presented with this stance, you might simply decide to *surrender*. You might look closely at the deal and conclude that it actually represents a good price. It may not be your perfect price, but it is one that you can accept today so you can close the deal and move on to making money elsewhere.

Sometimes you get lucky and the price that's offered is exactly what you're looking for, in which case surrendering isn't a bad thing. If you will never again deal with the other party and you don't need their goodwill, then you can be tough buying or selling—you don't need a negotiation, but there may just be some haggling over price, for example.

Arbitration is also an alternative to negotiation. The definition of arbitration is the resolution of conflict by an independent third party. However, by its nature, we all feel a certain loss of control over the outcome. The highest level of arbitration is when you go to court. "I don't agree with that pricing structure within the contract; I'll see you in court" or "You didn't deliver on time; I'll see what the judge has to say." That's an extreme form of arbitration. Other forms of arbitration and mediation will depend on the culture and business framework in whatever part of the world you are operating. Essentially, an independent third party reviews the evidence in the dispute and imposes a decision that is legally binding for both sides and is enforceable. In the United Kingdom, one such body is the Advisory, Conciliation and Arbitration Service (ACAS). The United States has the American Arbitration Association (AAA) and the National Arbitration Forum (NAF), among others. In the Middle East there is the Dubai International Arbitration Centre (DIAC) and others. Elsewhere in Asia, there is the China International Economic and Trade Arbitration Commission (CIETAC), the Japan Commercial Arbitration Association (JCAA), the Korean Commercial Arbitration Board (KCAB), the India Council of Arbitration, and many others.

Unlike court proceedings, arbitration and mediation are confidential and intended to be sufficiently flexible to meet the needs of the circumstances of an individual case. Construction and consumer disputes are commonly resolved by a type of arbitration known as adjudication, which is a process that may be used to resolve disputes without invoking what is likely to be a lengthy and expensive court procedure. An adjudicator will consider the summarized arguments of both parties and quickly make a decision designed to allow both parties to progress with their project or transaction. However, at the end of most forms of arbitration many parties feel that they have lost out, even if they've been awarded the decision. Most people feel they've had a loss because, at a minimum, there has been a loss of control.

Problem solving is the resolution of conflict by mutual agreement. No compromise is required in problem solving. Consider an example of a simple mathematical problem: what is 1×10? If we say the answer is 10, you would probably agree with us; we didn't need to compromise. However, let's extend that simple problem to the situation where a customer last year bought an item from you for $1,000 and now this year wants to buy ten items. The key question will be, what's your best price for a batch of ten? Well, your first stance may be that the total price is $1,000 \times 10$, which is $10,000, please. At that point, the customer may say that's not a problem they want to solve in that way—yes, they agree on the mathematics, but they want a bulk discount. They say they would be giving you ten times more business, so they want to pay only $8,000. At that point you need to decide whether this is a problem that needs solving or whether you are now entering a negotiation. You need to ask yourself whether you are prepared to compromise. If the customer indicates they will give you an order for all ten items today if you agree on a better price, then you've moved from problem solving into negotiation.

To summarize this section, we have seen that in negotiation we aim for a result of "win-win," but there are a few alternatives. We could try to dictate terms so that we win and the other party loses. We could surrender to their terms so that they win and we lose. We could both go to arbitration, but the chances are that we will both feel that we have lost. Finally, we could try problem solving in which case we can both win as long as we are both working on the same point of agreement. We should end by adding one more ancient strategy for resolving conflict: violence and warfare, a definite "lose-lose"!

In our experience, negotiation is the most flexible form of conflict resolution. It involves only the specific parties that have a "dog in this fight"—a genuine stake in the dispute. The parties can choose to define and shape the negotiation according to their specific circumstances and needs. They can agree on the agenda, decide where to negotiate, and elect to go public or to keep it all under wraps; the primary parties can decide whether there should be other participants or whether representatives and various expert advisors need to be involved. The probability of reaching a satisfactory resolution is increased because the parties can ensure that everyone who has a stake in the dispute can be consulted to ensure they are willing to participate. They can also agree on safeguards to minimize inequities in the negotiation process, such as an imbalance in power between the parties. In general, a negotiated resolution is a contract, even if it is not written down, and may therefore be enforced under the law of contracts. But the agreement may be void in the following circumstances: if it lacks consideration, is based on mutual mistakes, or was reached through duress or fraud (for example if one party misrepresented the law, lied about the facts, or otherwise deliberately deceived the other party in order to gain an advantage in the negotiation).

Negotiating Is Not Haggling

Many people who think about negotiation immediately focus on price. Good negotiators, while they have a handle on price, are more likely to be thinking of value. In commercial negotiation, value is an expression of how much better the customer's business goals can be met by the supplier's product or service rather than by the competition's. Experienced negotiators know that exploring relative values and the creation of value will give them a broader spectrum of activity and more negotiable elements as part of the overall deal. If you stick to price alone, you are simply haggling, not negotiating.

Our Four Negotiation Mantras

Our clients frequently ask us how best to recognize when the other party is prepared for negotiation. Sometimes, one party can begin a negotiation without the other party feeling that a negotiation has started. Our clients often ask how to distinguish between simply building initial rapport and the more substantial phases of negotiation, how they can be sure they should continue to negotiate, and how to know when it's time to reach a conclusion. To answer these questions, RDC has four negotiation mantras that are worth chanting to yourself, as shown in Figure 3-1.

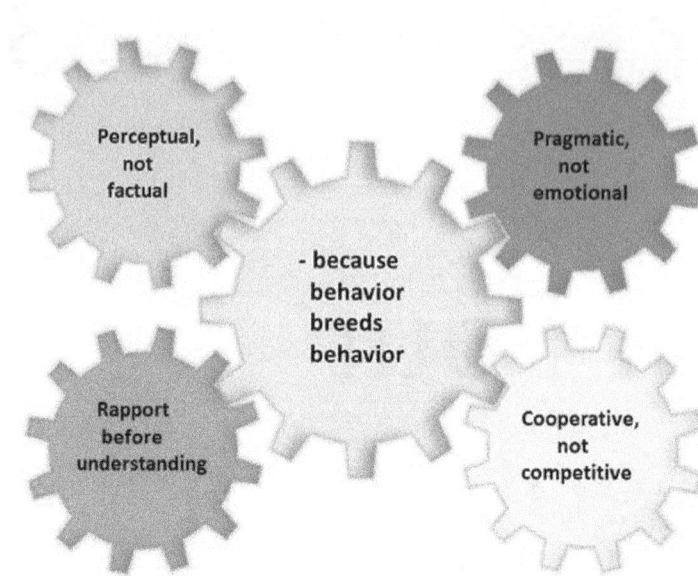

Figure 3-1. The RDC negotiation mantras

Mantra 1: Negotiation Is Perceptual, Not Factual

Negotiation is all about human interactions, so many people consider it to be an art rather than a science (some would say a black art). Perhaps there is a sliding scale where the opposite ends are labeled "art" and "science," but most negotiators agree that their expertise probably sits closer to the former than the latter. There are some aspects of a scientific discipline involved: some fundamental concepts and technical procedures have been researched and documented, and there are criteria and measurements that can be applied. Various aspects of negotiation can be tested, modeled, and debated, but there is no overarching scientific theory of negotiation. In the end, the critical dimension of complex human interaction means that negotiation is firmly perceptual rather than factual. If either party is insisting on a purely scientific, factual approach, then by definition they are probably not trying to negotiate. Put yourself in the position of a salesperson sitting across from a potential customer. You may find yourself with a huge spreadsheet and a pen in your hand and a calculator on the table, and you are continually referring to the facts of the deal. If so, you will probably find that the other party doesn't feel they are in a negotiation. Either they are most likely buying hard from you or they're trying to understand the position so that they can then buy well.

In a negotiation, both parties must feel a level of trust in each other and believe that this is a mutual resolution of conflict. Ideally, they can each have a true perception. However, if you try to force facts on people, they often get suspicious. You may feel that this is the best deal you've ever offered, and factually it might be correct. These might be the best credit terms you've ever given, the lowest price, or the most bells and whistles on the product. Then the other party says, "Yes, but I'm not comfortable with it; I don't like the way you presented it" or "I don't think you've gone far enough toward my requirements." Their perception then leads them to conclude that you are not really negotiating because you're just working on the cold facts.

People's perceptions can often be at odds with reality. When asked by researchers, many people said they anticipated great delight at the prospect of their favorite team winning a key event, but they revealed that the reality was a somewhat lesser elation. Conversely, the prospect of their team losing a key event was expected to upset them greatly, but the reality was not as bad as they had thought it would be. People also disclosed that they anticipated feeling a long, devastating depression if they were to be bereaved, but the reality for many was a quicker recovery than they expected. The anticipation of delight and the worry of impending disaster are both powerful perceptions that may not be fully grounded in factual reality. Research indicates that money does not necessarily bring as much lasting happiness as does networks of friends and family. A better self-awareness of your own goals and what will make you happy can help you in negotiation. Stray fears and greedy desires can bubble up even during the evaluation of cold facts, so be aware that negotiation is perceptual, not factual.

Mantra 2: Clear Yourself of Emotion and Be Pragmatic

When things go wrong in a corporate or private relationship, you have to stay pragmatic. There is little point just hoping for the world to be better tomorrow, but you can work toward making it better. Similarly, there is no point in wishing that the world was the same today as it was yesterday because that's gone; you can't change it. Both of those hopes and wishes are emotional engagements we all have. People look for justification and fair play and honesty (well, we can all hope we're going to get that eventually). However, pragmatically what we should do in every negotiation is focus on what's going on right now. If the other party says they're unhappy with the price, let's not get upset with them; let's explore why. If we are selling, it might be just that they don't have the money right now, or they didn't expect to spend that much. If we are buying, it might be that they have an irrational, emotional attachment to their asking price or they don't understand how far the market has recently fallen. No matter which side of the table we are on, it's now our job to work with the other party to help them understand the reality of the current situation.

Before a negotiation that is important to you, it is normal for you to feel anxious or even fearful. Similarly, the other party may be concerned or in contrast may be elated with the hope of achieving their objectives. In the initial stages, any miscommunication may result in anger. All these emotions are understandable and should be expected, but you have to compose yourself and don't allow your emotions to take control of your rational self. This doesn't mean you should try to ignore or suppress your emotions, merely that you should recognize them and learn how to handle them. Emotions can be useful in a negotiation, but only if you learn how to use them constructively rather allow yourself to be swamped by them. Make allowances for your own emotions and those of the other party. In many negotiations, when you are aware of your emotions but in control of them, they can be useful to help you recognize if you are on course or if you need to adjust your approach.

It's right for both parties to discuss their emotions—in a cool and rational manner. If it is difficult to do so, then try to express yourself as if you were describing an emotion in someone else. You will see later in this book that hostage negotiations are often initially characterized by intense emotions. This is for two reasons: lives may be directly at stake, and many hostage takers are driven by emotional anxieties and relationship problems. Their overt demands may be for a helicopter and a suitcase full of money, but they are often just seeking attention and respect. In any type of negotiation, patient listening and talking are crucial. Eventually this will help both parties to clear themselves of emotion and to be pragmatic. So, the mantra is to stay pragmatic, stay open-minded, and don't engage emotionally.

Mantra 3: Negotiation Is Cooperative, Not Competitive

Buying and selling is often competitive, but successful negotiation requires cooperation. The problem here is that buyers and salespeople are mostly recruited to be competitive people. It's quite an adversarial engagement in many cases. Getting the right price, getting the best deal, or getting it on your terms—all of these things are highly competitive activities. Therefore, you need to carefully distinguish between those times when you are buying and selling and those times when you are negotiating. You must learn how to switch from one mode to the other. You should develop the conscious skill of deciding when to drop your competitive mental state that is useful in buying or selling and instead engage your cooperative negotiation mode. If you learn how to do this, you will win more negotiated deals. Of course, it's not enough for individual sellers and buyers to do this; their organizations also need to provide a strategy and framework of processes to support negotiations to the same extent as they support the processes of buying and selling. When it's time to switch to negotiation mode, the whole organization has to support and enable the cooperative approach. We'll develop this important idea in a later chapter.

There is a similar struggle to switch from competitive mode to cooperative mode when lawyers need to negotiate on behalf of their clients. Lawyers like to win cases; they are competitive. For trial, they prepare arguments and stratagems for how they will win over the jury by proving that the other side is absolutely wrong and they are completely right. But in a negotiation, the lawyer needs to switch from trial mode into a more cooperative mode. Instead of trying to win on every disputed issue, they have to learn how to compromise in return for what their client wants and needs.

Fortunately, it seems that over tens of thousands of years human nature has gradually developed our ability to switch from being competitive to cooperative—and back again if necessary! Scientific experts tell us that during our early evolution we were loving, protective, and cooperative only toward our immediate family and friends, but that over many generations we slowly evolved the behavior of extending our cooperation to other members of our society. In fact, in the few remaining bands of hunter-gatherers today, we see interesting behavior that is relevant to negotiation. Many hunts are unsuccessful, and some hunters will have nothing to bring home to eat. However, a skilled and successful hunter may be able to acquire in one day much more than can be consumed by his immediate family. In the absence of technology to store the surplus, the best strategy is to give it away to other people in the group on the understanding that this behavior will be reciprocated when fortunes are reversed over the next few days. If any individual were to renege on this arrangement and fail to share their future surplus, then that person would be subject to social retaliation, poor marriage prospects, or potential exclusion. Basically, uncooperative behavior has been selected against while cooperative behavior has been reinforced over many generations. In the earliest communities, such cooperation encompassed only close members of our band or tribe. Later, we gradually learned to extend our cooperation to broader groups of people in tribal associations to make it easier to hunt and forage. Much later, we were able to adopt a more sedentary lifestyle, eventually living in settlements with large numbers of other people by extending to them a sort of honorary membership of our trusted family group. However, when we engage in this cooperative behavior, it seems we do not do it unconditionally. Research indicates that when we are considering whether a stranger is worthy of being included in our trusted circle, we tend to initially give them the benefit of the doubt, allowing them to benefit from our cooperation, and then see how well they reciprocate our good behavior. If they are fair and reciprocate in kind, without being mean or trying to cheat, then we learn to trust them more and continue to treat them well. On the other hand, if they do not reciprocate our cooperative behavior, then we treat them as cheats and switch our approach from cooperative to competitive. Today, a good negotiator is aware of these innate behaviors in people and seeks to harness them to the benefit of both parties. A professional negotiator will start by being cooperative in order to encourage the other party to switch out of their competitive mode and engage their cooperative spirit.

Some people have to overcome their impression that in all negotiations there must be a winner and a loser. These people feel that even when both parties gain benefits, one will benefit more than the other, and therefore there is still a loser! People with this extreme competitive style can, with guidance, learn how to see an exchange of concessions as a strength rather than a weakness. With practice, they can aim for an agreement that creates benefits for both parties, above and beyond those that either could generate in isolation. Some of us are naturally competitive, and it is thoroughly understandable if you find yourself continually reining yourself in, but that's what you must do. Try not to paint the other party into a corner, try not to get them to make assumptions, and try not to get them to commit themselves too soon. Work on cooperation as much as you can. You may come to realize that the other party also wants to be cooperative but perhaps feels you have some conflicting interests over exactly how to cooperate. There is an old saying that you catch more flies with honey than you do with vinegar. That's why in this mantra we're looking for cooperation and not competition.

Mantra 4: Rapport First, Understanding Second

It takes time to build rapport. Many people, because of nerves, enthusiasm, competition, or aggression, try to cut to the chase in a negotiation. These people want to get all the facts out on the table, "letting the dog see the rabbit." People often try to reach for understanding first. This is a mistake. If you want a "win-win" resolution by mutual compromise, the other party needs to have a certain level of trust and respect for you. You don't get that by cutting to the chase. You do get it by listening and generating rapport.

That doesn't necessarily mean talking about their kids, about the dog, about the weekend, or about the football. You don't need to talk about your journey or how nicely their office is decorated. You generate rapport by following the previous three mantras. Stay sensitive to the other party's perception of the conflict you are trying to resolve. Refrain from immediately disputing their interpretation of the facts. Stay sensitive to their views and emotions around the issues and don't allow your own emotions to overcome your logic. Listen carefully and frequently check your understanding. Be pragmatic about why you're both there and don't try to build a case that makes your life easier. Keep your competitive self in check. Stay cooperative from the beginning. You don't have to give anything away, but, at the start, a bit of cooperation and understanding about the pragmatic view and the other party's legitimate right to a perception will help you to build rapport. In hostage negotiations, there is often a huge amount of effort and time put into this early phase of communicating, demonstrating that you are listening, showing empathy, and gradually building rapport. This has to be done before you can begin to understand the other party's position, and it is essential before the other party is ready to allow their emotions to cool down so they can begin to grasp the reality of the hostage situation. There are often close parallels between these aspects of hostage negotiations and the early phases of commercial negotiations.

To check how well you are performing against the negotiation mantras, you should ask yourself whether you are being perceptual, pragmatic, and cooperative. Are you trying to generate rapport with this other party? Keep in mind that behavior breeds behavior. If you don't listen to them, they won't listen to you. If you aggressively cut to the chase, so will the other party. If you are competitive and try to slice pieces off for yourself, so will they. If you are emotional, crying, shouting, and arguing, you will generate an emotional atmosphere, and the other party will respond in kind. Finally, if you don't take account of their perceptions—if you appear aloof and just stick to the facts— they will think that's how you want to do it, and they will not take any account of your perception. The other party's behavior is bred by your behavior, and the danger is that your behavior will reflect theirs unless you consciously rise above it.

So, negotiation is the voluntary and systematic exploration of both parties' interests with the objective of agreeing a mutually acceptable compromise that resolves their conflict—that's "win-win." There are four other alternatives to negotiation to resolve a conflict: dictating terms, surrendering, arbitration, and problem solving. And there are the negotiation mantras: perceptual, not factual; pragmatic, not emotional; cooperative, not competitive; rapport first, understanding second. Also remember that behavior breeds behavior. If you keep all this in mind, you will develop a personal philosophy of negotiation that makes the rules easier to understand and to apply in practice.

Overview of the Five Phases of Negotiation

You're now ready to learn about the types of activities that go on in all negotiations. Before we cover in depth the behavior in any one part of commercial negotiation, we'll break down the process into five overall phases, as shown in Figure 4-1.

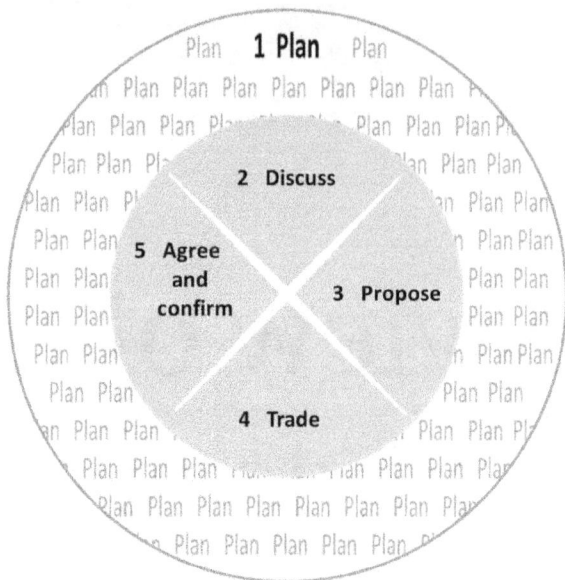

Figure 4-1. The five phases of negotiation

The planning phase is so important that it's shown as completely surrounding the other phases. There are two reasons for this. First, it is the initial phase, and you should not get into any negotiation without having done the appropriate degree of planning; second, you will almost always go through cycles of refined planning as you progress from one phase to the next. If you are expecting your negotiation to be simple and straightforward, with few serious consequences if it goes wrong, then a quick plan may suffice, followed by a rapid progression through the other phases. You might do this in minutes. At the opposite extreme, you may have a critical negotiation with livelihoods, if not lives, depending on the outcome. In these circumstances you may need several weeks or months in the planning phase, followed by a discussion phase, during which you break off for extended periods to review and refine your planning. Each of the subsequent phases of propose and trade may be equally extended in time if the negotiation is complex and if the consequences of a failure to reach a resolution warrant the investment of time and effort. You may need to temporarily break off negotiations with the other party at any and all phases in order to check the progress and plan how to adjust your tactics as necessary to achieve your objectives, before you can conclude with the fifth phase, agree and confirm. Let's now walk through, in some detail, what happens in each of the five phases.

Phase 1: Plan

As you can see from Figure 4-1, planning is the first and most critical phase of negotiation for ensuring a successful outcome—and it doesn't stop there! Planning permeates every stage of negotiation, and you should review and refine your plans during and in between every other phase of the negotiation. This is called the *cycle of planning*. The first planning cycle starts with asking yourself whether you and the other party have any credible alternatives to negotiation.

What's the Alternative?

A critical component of your planning effort should be to quantify which party is most at risk. Who stands to lose most if the negotiation fails to reach a resolution of the conflict? Consider what the potential consequences are for you and for the other party in winning or losing this deal. You need to evaluate the alternatives to negotiation that may be available both to you and to the other party. You also need to find relevant data that will help you to understand how much power the other party will be able to wield in this negotiation. Clearly, your job is going to be a lot harder if the other party has a viable alternative to reaching a resolution with you. Conversely, your job is going to be a lot easier if they know that you have a credible alternative to dealing with them.

Competitor Analysis

Competitor analysis is extremely important for both buyers and sellers. If you are in sales, ensure you know exactly who your current competitors are and what they are offering compared to your own products and services. You need to know precisely how similar and how different their offerings and deals are compared to yours. What are their price lists? What discounts have they been giving? What are their payment terms? What's included in the specification of their product or service compared to yours? All this will help you to protect yourself from the other party making either valid comparisons or trying to "cherry-pick" features of deals from several of your competitors and exaggerate these into a firm offer by an unnamed rival. You need to have better intelligence about your competition than your prospect does.

The reverse is true if you are buying. You should invest the time needed to research and explore several potential suppliers and their product offerings. Investigate their qualifications, credentials, trade associations, and so on. Speak to their other customers, and if possible, go to visit a couple that are in the most similar situation to yourself. In any type of negotiation, you should research with due diligence and determine what it is that differentiates one deal from another.

Due Diligence

Over the past couple of decades, we have heard the phrase *due diligence* being used all too often to mean conducting research and analysis only to the minimum extent that you can get away with! In contrast, our view of due diligence is that you need to research, analyze, and plan to the depth, breadth, and standards that are commensurate with the rewards and risks in each negotiation. Every dollar you spend in planning will pay you back tenfold in the end. From the outset, you should focus your planning on the creation of value, which is an expression of how much better the customer's business goals can be met by the supplier's product or service rather than by the competition's.

Information

One of the most important dimensions that you need to plan in detail relates to the search for pertinent information that you will put to good use in the negotiation. Of course, for certain types of negotiation such as mergers and acquisitions, this intelligence gathering will be of critical importance and will be conducted professionally. Even for what you may consider to be an everyday negotiation, good research can make a huge difference to your success. One note of caution is to avoid being fed bogus information that may have been deliberately planted or leaked by the other party.

In some types of negotiation, there may be little opportunity for gathering much useful information in advance, such as in crisis negotiations triggered by threatened self-harm or the taking of hostages. However, let's focus on the example of a complex commercial negotiation for which you have sufficient time to prepare. Aim to compile a pack of resources that you will be taking into the negotiation with you. For straightforward and low-risk negotiations, this could simply be a mental list. For other more complex and important negotiations, you should create a formal, written set of comprehensive briefing notes and other resources. You may need a preliminary bout of general research to prepare the groundwork, followed by specific searches for publicly available information on the other party and the subjects at stake in the deal. You may be able to find useful background on the other party's activities and, if relevant, their competitors' history and current direction. You should try to determine their motives and methods of business. What are their major categories of cost? Where are their mainstream profits generated? If you are buying, make sure you look for information to help you understand the supplier's business drivers. When do their financial periods end? What pressures may they be under in their business? If you are selling, determine how your proposal may fit in with the prospect's long-term goals and short-term objectives.

Try to find out as much as possible about the individuals you will be negotiating with. Perhaps you can find out their negotiating style and something about their background and interests. Will there be people from the Finance function in their negotiating team? Will Operations be represented? Perhaps there are one or two technical specialists or lawyers and so on. Build up a picture of these various stakeholders and their interests.

If you are selling, make sure you have an official written price list in your pack of resources that you will be taking with you into the negotiation. Written list prices carry far more weight than the spoken word and are less likely to be challenged. Similarly, if you have relevant policies and contracts, make sure you take the formal-looking copies with you. If you are buying, you may also have relevant policies and contracts to take with you. Of course, you will not allow yourself to be awed by your suppliers' formal list prices! Whatever type of negotiation you are planning and no matter which side of the table you will be on, you would do well to search for any independent standards, objective guidelines, or rules of precedent that both parties may be able to respect. If you find such relevant standards, they could be used as a yardstick in your negotiation and may be a good lever for you to use to adjust the stance taken by the other party.

You should then dedicate a large proportion of the time you spend in planning to define what information you still need. Many people are relatively poor at planning the questions they need to ask. People sometimes think they can simply wing it. They've negotiated so many times before that they think they won't be surprised this time. Our recommendation is to try to find ten questions that will unearth the most important information that you will need to know—and write them down. Don't stop at three or four questions; force yourself to find at least ten.

The Agenda

Research by social psychologists has indicated that the mutual effectiveness of negotiation is generally increased if the communication channels and the procedures to be followed are agreed on in advance by both parties. When the ground rules are not agreed on in advance, this often leads to competitive rather than cooperative behavior. Before the negotiation begins, the mutual identification of the issues to be discussed produces better results than unilateral planning. Research indicates that if the parties can agree on a structure for the negotiation, they manage to get closer together on the issues and are more cooperative, usually reaching agreement more often and more rapidly than is otherwise possible.

As part of your planning, you should consider who is to set the agenda for the negotiation. People who don't negotiate often can feel tempted to create their own agenda quickly, before the other party can load their own issues into their agenda. In our experience, there are a couple of better ways of handling this. If the other party insists on producing an agenda, relax and let them take the initiative. Use this to start to build rapport. In any case, the agenda they produce may disclose to you some of their key interests and values. In other circumstances, it may be best for both parties to draft an agenda with the aim of discussing and then sharing an agreed-upon final version. At the opposite extreme, you may find that the other party may try to insist on a formal, jointly signed agreement on general principles and perhaps a letter of intent before the start of any negotiation. We have seen instances where a separate negotiation was needed to agree on such principles before the start of the main event! Beware of such devices because they are probably designed to create an advantage for the other party, and in the late stages of the negotiation, you may find yourself accused of departing from the spirit of the "prenuptial."

Once the agenda is agreed on, you should make time to practice how you will defend yourself against the arguments likely to be put forward by the other party. Assign one of your team to take on this role and make sure they give you a good grilling so you have the best opportunity to rehearse the tactics you will employ in the real negotiation. The planning phase is so important that we will expand on all this shortly and provide the RDC ten-point plan to help you achieve successful negotiations.

Phase 2: Discuss

No matter how much good planning has been done in the first phase of negotiation, the second phase is critical because it may be the first time that the parties have actually had a discussion. Here is the opportunity to make sure that the issues are clear and for both parties to look each other in the eye, listen, and look out for signals coming from the other party. Good negotiators will often go from their planning phase to make a rapid guerrilla raid into the discussion phase and then quickly bug out back into planning. Because they've begun to ask the questions they have carefully planned and they've had some conversations that have provided valuable intelligence about the other party, they can now perform more relevant and effective planning. Once this new cycle of planning is completed, they can reconvene the discussion, as depicted by the arrows in Figure 4-2.

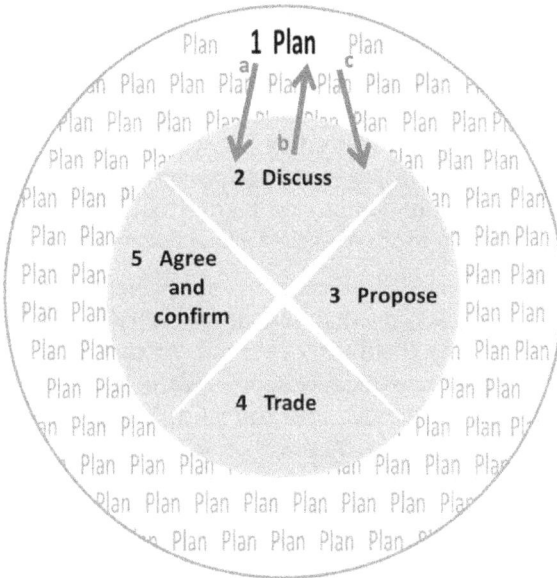

Figure 4-2. From planning to discussing, back to planning, and then to discussing again

Even after this refined planning, the first thing a good negotiator will do in the next discussion is reconfirm in summary all the things they think they've learned—to make sure they've got it right. They will also spend time testing the other party's understanding of the discussion. Poor negotiators may be tempted to allow misinterpretations to continue if these appear to be to their advantage, and they may avoid clarifying ambiguous points in case the other party disagrees.

The discussion phase is essential to set the tone of a negotiation so that the parties can build trust and begin to share information openly and honestly. Our experience is that in turn this will enable the parties to jointly create more value that, in a commercial context, is an expression of how much better the customer's business goals can be met by the supplier's product or service rather than by the competition's. Cooperation is more beneficial to both parties than competition. Of course, people will be concerned about not divulging commercial secrets, given the risk that such information could be misused. However, being as open and honest as possible can open the floodgates to the possibilities that would have remained unavailable to either party acting in isolation. Even when negotiations take place between colleagues in one business, it can be hard for some people to accept that being open and honest is usually the best strategy. Therefore, don't just accept at face value a declaration of an interest. You should probe to understand why this interest is so important to the other party. Do they seem to have strong underlying beliefs that would feed this interest? Are they really placing a high value on this interest, or is this just a "decoy"—a false interest that they may be hoping to agree to forego, later in the trading phase, in exchange for a high-value concession from you? The discussion phase is important to test whether both parties feel sufficiently confident to curb their natural competitiveness and engage their cooperation mode to gain mutual advantage.

Sometimes people's desired outcomes are set naively. You need to use the discussion phase to seek out what the other party's target outcomes may be, with a view to helping them achieve them. At the same time, don't force yourself naively to seek your ideal outcome without having any grounds for setting that as a realistic objective. We can all suffer from tunnel vision: when we see only the one outcome that we want and so we aim straight for it regardless of what is being said or done around us. In a negotiation, you need to understand your own interests that are driving you toward your desired outcome because there may be many ways in which your values and interests can be satisfied apart from the single target that you have in mind. Similarly, the other party may initially be blinkered to other possibilities: they may be taking an inflexible stance even though there may be other ways of satisfying their interests that you will find more acceptable. Therefore, your job is to remain open to other ways of satisfying your interests and to suggest ways in which the other party might satisfy their interests without damaging you in the process. You need to be patient and avoid attacking the other party and their declarations. If they attack you, you need to bite your tongue and avoid escalating the argument.

The useful "80/20 rule" is to listen more and talk less, even if the other party is droning on and you feel you are not getting any meaningful information. It's better for the other party to be droning on, if you are listening, than for you to be doing this. You may be tempted to interrupt, but resist and keep listening. The danger is that if you indulge yourself, you will miss key points in the discussion, and you will allow the other party to pick out the nuggets of signals from you. If you interrupt the other party and they feel you are being impolite, they may punish you in one way or another. For example, they may not go back to what they were saying. They may have just been at the point when they were about to tell you where the key was that opened the door to the path that leads to the holy grail—your ideal outcome. However, when you ask them to resume, they may say they have lost track, forgotten what they were about to say, or simply shrug and say it doesn't matter now.

Of course, when we recommend that you listen more, we mean active listening, not just passive listening. Your body language and eye contact will be important to reassure the other party that you are actually in receive mode.

Sit up and show them that you are interested. At appropriate intervals, check that you grasp their points by summarizing to them what you think they've said. Try saying, "Let's see if I've got this right; you seem to be saying that...." This shows them you are really trying to listen, and it gives them the chance to adjust your understanding if they feel you haven't quite got it right. You should be aware of the danger of simply using the time when the other party is talking to formulate your own next utterances, rather than actually absorbing what is being said to you. If the other party appears reluctant to talk, encourage them with open questions to get them going. You don't want to turn into a "nodding dog," but occasional nods of encouragement and muttering "Oh, yeah" and raising your eyebrows may help to keep them talking. Once they are talking, resist the temptation to interrupt or finish their sentences for them, and restrain the tendency we all have to look for lateral connections so we can point out mutual interests. Anything you say could sidetrack the other party and prevent them from telling you something important. Having said all that, don't go to the other extreme and sit in frigid silence. After all, this is a discussion, so you need to open up enough to have a genuine conversation without seeming to dominate.

People are often tempted to give away concessions in the discussion phase, but at such an early stage this would simply breed a concession mentality. It is understandable for you to be tempted to give away what we call a free gift. It may seem to you that this gift doesn't cost you anything, and you may think that it will get the ball rolling. However, if you give them a concession at this early stage without obtaining anything in return, you will teach them how to ask you for more until you have nothing left to trade when you get into the trading phase. We are not yet in the trading phase, so do not consider any free gifts at this early stage.

One of your objectives should be to build up a comprehensive list of all the interests and elements of the deal from the other party's perspective. You will want to avoid progressing into the propose and trade phases of the negotiation and thinking you have a deal, only to discover in the final stages that the other party is raising new interests, raising new elements, and demanding new concessions from you.

Consider the boundary between the negotiation phases of discuss and propose. One of the key concepts is the use of signals. For example, the other party may say "Under *normal* circumstances we wouldn't pay for those vouchers up front." Does this mean that under the right circumstances they may be prepared to do so? Another example may be if they say "We *regularly* ask for this money up front" or that "Our *standard* terms are for the money up front." They haven't said they always ask for the money up front or that the only way they can deal with this is by having the money up front. This could be a signal that they may be prepared to move away from their standard terms if you are willing to change some key element such as price, specification, currency, liability, and so on. However, they are choosing their words carefully so that they are not lying, but they are trying to give you the impression that they have little flexibility on this deal. Your challenge is to listen carefully and decipher the signals.

There are two distinct types of signal—leaked and intentional. A leaked signal is when the other party says something they didn't mean to reveal. That's why it's so important for you to listen carefully because you may hear something to your advantage that they didn't mean to disclose. An intentional signal is when the discussion phase is correctly used to transmit signals about the requirements of either party. It is appropriate for you to plan what information you want to intentionally transmit during the discussion phase. Sometimes information is provided in an overt manner and at other times more subtly. For example, a salesperson may say, "This is our list price, our ticket price." This may indicate that they can offer a lower price if the deal is right. Similarly, the salesperson may say "We couldn't possibly deliver *that* quantity in *that* timescale." Often this is a signal that they could deliver a reduced quantity in the required timescale or the desired quantity in a longer timescale. Your job in the discussion phase is to work out what they could be implying. What do they mean—and what may they have left out?

This could be more difficult than you imagine because people often only see and hear the signals they are expecting and miss the types of signal they are not expecting. They may not be on alert for or preconditioned to receive certain types of signal. For example, if you are a salesperson and are conditioned to be looking for an opportunity and you hear somebody say "10 to 12 percent discount," you are likely to interpret this as an opportunity to sell at a 10 percent discount. On the other hand, if you are a buyer and are conditioned to be looking for the maximum value for money and you hear somebody say "10 to 12 percent discount," you are likely to interpret this as an offer to sell to you at a 12 percent discount. Some people act as if they were deaf to your discussion points unless these confirm their own position, or they appear to be deaf to your points until there is one that they can pounce on and rip to shreds—so make sure you don't do this!

People are also prone to interpret signals in different ways depending on whether they are expecting a threat or an opportunity. The lessons to be learned from this are to always keep an open mind, listen and watch carefully, and summarize what you think you have heard so that the other party can confirm or correct your understanding.

Phase 3: Propose

From the discussion phase you can readily go back into another cycle of planning to check the signals, consider what you have learned, review and update your plans, and then proceed into the propose phase, as depicted by the arrows in Figure 4-3.

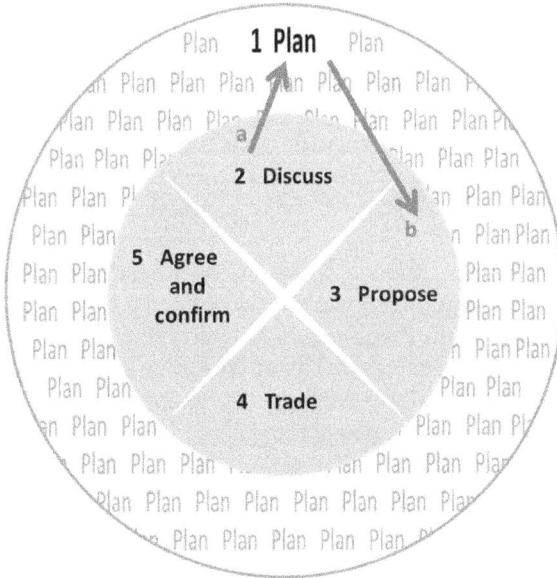

Figure 4-3. From discuss through plan to propose

This Is Not the Same as a Sales Proposal

In a negotiation, the term *propose* or *proposal* should not be confused with the same words used in the context of simply buying and selling. If you are a buyer, you will often issue a request for proposal (RFP) to invite potential suppliers to bid for your business. If you are a salesperson, you may feel you have spent all too many long hours creating your proposals in response to RFPs. Our key message to buyers and sellers is to buy and sell hard and avoid the need to compromise that is inherent in a negotiation. When you are buying and selling, the proposal aims to communicate three different types of information about the product or service. It may describe the features of the product—the facts about what it is and its specifications. It may also describe what generic advantages these features may confer on anyone who may want to use the product.

Finally and most importantly, the sales proposal describes how the product or service specifically satisfies the customer's requirements and generates real value for the customer in the form of tangible benefits. From the salesperson's perspective, the ideal would be for their product to be uniquely able to deliver these specific, valuable benefits to the customer when other products can't. This forms the seller's value proposition, which is the solution to the buyer's requirements; that is what is meant by a proposal in the context of buying and selling.

What Is Meant by Propose in a Negotiation

In the propose phase of a negotiation, you could hear the following exploratory dialogue: "If instead of giving you vouchers, I were to consider the possibility of giving you a hard discount, what payment terms could you consider moving to?" This type of dialogue is merely exploratory and tentative and therefore belongs in the propose phase. In contrast, during the trade phase of the negotiation, you would hear a definitive offer to trade, such as "I will give you a 20 percent discount if you pay in full with your order." These examples illustrate some key differences between the phases of propose and trade. RDC uses the metaphor of a jellyfish to represent how you can create more effective proposals during your negotiations.

Imagine that as a buyer you craft the perfect deal. It has many elements: the lowest price, the longest credit terms, the most extensive security of relationship, and the minimum adverse contractual terms. Or if you are a salesperson, you craft your perfect deal: the highest price, the basic product, the shortest credit terms, and completion of the deal in time for a good bonus! This is your well-shaped jellyfish, just like the ones washed up on the beach that many of us will remember from our childhood. You hand this over to the other party and watch in dismay as he gets his playful five-year-olds to come and stomp all over your perfect jellyfish of a proposal. It may change shape many times during the negotiation, but if you have constructed it carefully, the basic integrity of the deal should be intact. You should still find it acceptable, although not as pretty anymore.

Most negotiators make a single proposal at any one time, and in most but not all circumstances, this is what we recommend. We will describe later in the book the occasional situations when it is appropriate to propose two or more alternatives at the same time. This way, you may learn a bit more about the values and priorities of the other party as they sift through the options you have proposed. The elements of your proposals that they like and dislike may indicate the most fruitful areas for potential trades. On the other hand, if you only ever make a single proposal and it is rejected, you may not learn much additional information to help the negotiation, but at least you don't run the risk of the other party pouncing on the multiple elements that you have exposed. You will see when we discuss the ten golden rules of negotiation that the eighth rule is to watch out for the "salami" effect.

The analogy here is that your whole negotiation package with all its various elements is seen as the complete salami. The danger is that if you allow the other party to see the details of what's in the many slices of your total negotiation package, they may try to pick and choose the slices that they like best and leave you with an unsatisfactory, unprofitable, and unpalatable deal. That's the salami effect. You may have to reveal some of your salami slices if the other party insists, but only reveal the salami when necessary and do so only to the minimum extent demanded. If you judge that the situation requires you to make two or more proposals at the same time, then do so carefully. Even if the other party asks you for as many choices as possible to help them make an informed decision, if you propose a dozen options, they are likely to feel inundated, which will cause annoyance and damage the deal.

Sometimes you may hear the other party try to make a proposal, but they fall back into the trap of simply re-stating the stance they have taken, without giving you any room to maneuver toward a solution that satisfies the underlying values and interests of both parties. If this happens, then you need to exit from the proposal phase and loop back into the discussion. If the other party simply repeats their stance, summarize what you believe they have told you about their interests and ask them if you've got it right; then ask, "How would the stance you've described actually result in your interests being satisfied?" There are a number of open questions you could ask at this point, just to get them talking and ideally thinking about the difference between the stance they're taking and the interests they are pursuing, such as "Why are you so keen on that stance?" You are going to need to apply all your communication skills to the situation—and try to remain logical and calm.

During the propose phase, you may find that you enter into a detailed debate over some element of the proposal. Of course, you will want to persuade the other party to accept your proposal, and you will be keen to provide many reasons why they should agree. However, you should be aware of the danger of going through a long list of reasons. Instinctively, you will be inclined to start with your strongest points first, but as the long list progresses, your points will inevitably get weaker and weaker. The other party will forget your earlier, strongest arguments, and your confidence will wane. In our experience, the best way to avoid this is to have no more than three points on your list. Start with a strong point, follow it up with the weakest of the three, and then end with your most compelling. Similarly, if you need to refute a claim by the other party, don't try to deliver an exhaustive list of all your points of disagreement. It may be best to simply present your strongest point and then wait to see whether anyone can undermine it before you call in your reserves.

A tactic to be wary of is when the other party constructs a proposal containing an element that they insist is vitally important to them but it is blatantly one to which you could never agree. They may be expecting you to reject this proposal just so they can follow up with a second more realistic proposal in the hope that you will feel stressed and guilty and perhaps more inclined to compromise.

You may also come across another tactic that the other party can adopt when you are presenting them with your proposal. At the point when you reach the key element of price, they physically flinch as if in shock. It's difficult to do this convincingly, so you may want to congratulate them on their acting ability! Their intention is to make you think that your proposal was so far removed from their expectations that you now feel the need to make immediate concessions. You will resist this, of course, and will either ignore the tactic or ask them why they looked surprised and what it was they were expecting. This brings you both back into the discussion phase to talk about their unrealistic expectations and to refocus away from price. If you are in sales, then talk about your value proposition: how much better their business goals can be met by your product or service rather than by any alternative. If you are buying, go back over all the other elements of your proposal, apart from price, to reinforce the commitment you have to conclude the deal now if they can agree to your proposal.

Phase 4: Trade

This is the beating heart of negotiation. Remember that negotiation is all about compromise. The trading phase is when you actually get down to deciding which compromises you are willing to give in exchange for the compromises that the other party is willing to trade, as shown in Figure 4-4.

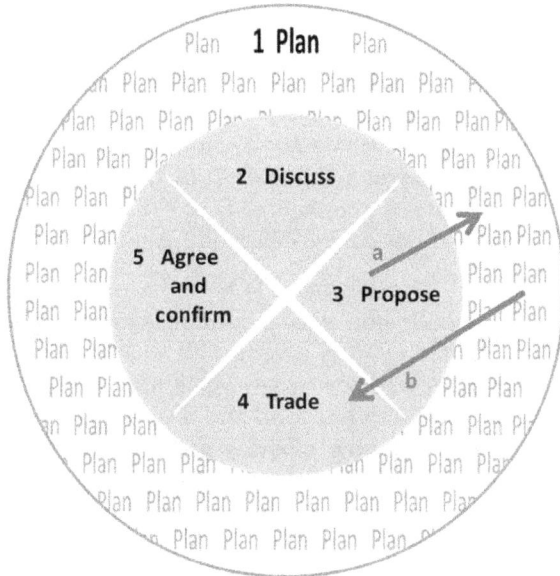

Figure 4-4. From propose through plan to trade

The arrows in Figure 4-4 show the simplified route from the propose phase, probably with an additional planning cycle, and then into the trade phase. However, the route can be more complicated. If the trade is not agreed on, you may go back into planning and back into discussion before you can be confident of returning to the propose and trade phases once more.

In many negotiations, we have found that the other party often wants what we are prepared to trade and that we want what the other party is willing to trade. However, there are some dangers you need to avoid. In the heat of negotiation, there are physical aspects to be aware of—adrenalin may be flowing, and you may be feeling over-confident. Beware of giving something away that you didn't mean to. Also, beware of naively believing a declaration of a tradable interest. You should probe to understand how valuable this interest is to the other party. They may be placing what they genuinely feel to be a high value on this interest, or they may be planting this decoy as a false interest that they may be planning to trade in exchange for a high-value concession from you.

In the planning phase you will have invested time and effort considering each negotiable element of the deal that you are willing to trade. During the discussion phase you will have probed what the other party really wants. In the propose phase you may have tentatively explored what they might be willing to exchange and how they value the concessions you may be willing to make. Now you are ready to ask yourself, for each of these potential concessions, what we call the *three trading questions* (3TQ): What is it going to cost me? What is it worth to the other party? What do I want in return?

To illustrate the benefit of using the 3TQ, we have a true-life story about one of our relatives, Geoff, who was a London taxi driver for most of his life. The Cabmen's Shelter Fund is a venerable charity that for well over a century has built and operated shelters—which look like large green garden sheds—to provide cabbies with hot food and drinks at moderate prices. The dozen remaining shelters are now officially protected buildings. Geoff often frequented a particular shelter and became friendly with the manager who it turned out lived quite close to Geoff's house. In the dead of night, when Geoff was about to head for home, he would drop in at the shelter to see whether the manager needed a "free" lift home. Later, this was extended to include the manager's daughter who often needed a lift into the city at the start of Geoff's long shift. In return for these lifts, Geoff's tab at the shelter was simply wiped off the slate each week. For many years until they both retired, both men benefited from their arrangement because they both understood that when trading concessions, it is important to find answers to the three trading questions.

- What is it going to cost me?
- What is it worth to the other party?
- What do I want in return?

When you are negotiating, these three questions will help you to evaluate both sides so that you can understand what could possibly be traded. Rookies and poor negotiators focus primarily on the price. Good negotiators know that there may be dozens or even hundreds of negotiable elements in a deal: quantity, specification, credit terms, currency, delivery schedules, decommissioning, training, maintenance, support, access to resources, research and development, key staff, warranty, liability, licenses, royalties, and many more. Don't get stuck on price. To trade successfully, you need to be able to determine the cost to you of what you are willing to give away, you need to know how much the other party values your concession, and you must decide what you want in return from the other party. For example, one element of the deal may cost you $1,000 to give away but may represent a value of $5,000 to the other party. This is what we call a lever. Of course, what you want in return is something worth at least $5,000 to you—and wouldn't it be a good "win-win" if the cost of this to the other party was only $1,000?

A simple example of this was a client who had some property adjoining a small farm. Developers bought the land and demolished the mid-eighteenth century farmhouse in order to build three or four executive homes on the site. However, to get the top price for these, a little bit more space was required. Our clients were willing to sell the developer a small segment of their land but were unsure about a fair price. We used the RDC ten-point plan, did some research, and entered negotiations. The resultant deal was for the extra profit projected at $120,000 to be shared equally by both parties, but for only half the sum, $30,000, to be paid in cash, half in advance and half on completion. The remaining $30,000 of value to our client was to be in the form of building work to our client's property that the developer could perform at marginal cost because the labor, equipment, and materials were already engaged on the site.

When you seem to be reaching the end of the trade phase, beware of the other party asking for one last concession to clinch the deal. Research indicates that most concessions are made right at the end of the negotiation. If you naively agree, you will probably find that yet another last concession is needed, and so on. In the earlier phases, you should have obtained a comprehensive list of all the genuine interests and elements of the deal. If new issues are coming to light now, you should return to the original list and ask why this new requirement was not mentioned earlier. Treat the new item as you would any negotiable element and decide what it would cost you, what it is worth to the other party, and what you want in return. Make sure you "empty the bucket" by asking specifically if there are any more issues still to be discussed before the deal is finalized.

Phase 5: Agree and Confirm

In a commercial context, sellers and buyers often learn how best to close a transaction. Many of these techniques are useful at the end of a negotiation, but there are differences to look out for. Clearly, the first step will be to check whether the objectives you set for yourself while planning the negotiation have actually been achieved. You need to be sure that now is the time to stop trading. To do this, you should return into another cycle of planning, ideally a quick one, before you agree and confirm the deal, as shown in Figure 4-5.

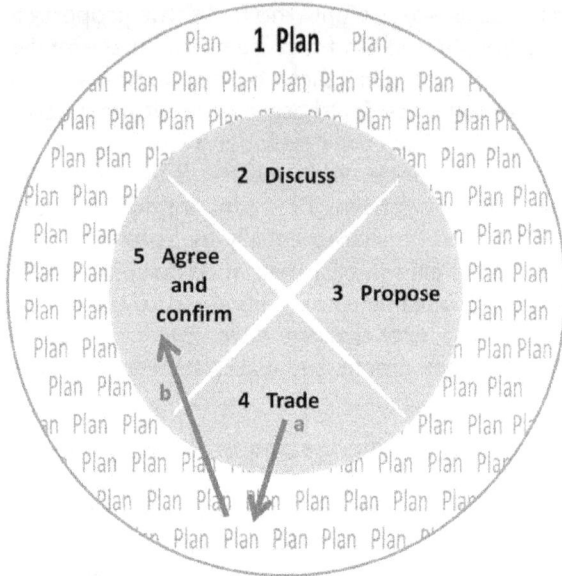

Figure 4-5. From trade into agree and confirm

Once you are sure your objectives have been met and you can stop negotiating, you can seek to close using one of the following techniques:

- Summarize and ask whether you have a deal. In most instances, this is a low-risk closing technique because the other party can easily say yes. If they say no or "let me think about it," you still haven't lost because you can loop back into the planning phase and then try another approach. The only caution to exercise in any close is that the other party perceives that you want to finish and get away and may try to trade your exit in exchange for you making another concession.

- Offer a final concession on the condition that this will enable you to now agree on the deal. In most instances, this is a medium-risk closing technique. The risk is higher than in the first example because you are now limiting your options in the event that the other party fails to agree. Your credibility would be damaged if you tried again to add one more "final" concession!

- Offer a choice of two alternative concessions on the condition that this will enable you to now agree on the deal. This is a high-risk closing technique not least because the other party could demand both concessions now that they know you are at least willing to concede either.

- Deliver an ultimatum. One example could simply be that this is your final position, take it or leave it. This is a very high-risk closing technique. You can't be bluffing when you issue such an ultimatum. If it is rejected, you must be willing to walk away from the deal despite all the hard work you have invested in it.

The other party may not accept, no matter which closing technique you select. You may need to loop back into a little bit of planning, then more discussion, and perhaps revised proposals until the trade is agreed on. For example, if you are selling, the buyer may say your product is exactly what they want and they would like to do business with you but your price is simply too high. You will want to focus on value rather than price, perhaps by asking whether the budget can be adjusted to take into account the future benefit flows from the deal. Remind them how much better their business goals can be met by your product or service rather than by the competition's. You could try asking by exactly how much the price is too high and follow up with, "If we could move substantially toward that figure, would you be willing to sign here and now?" This should help you to discover if this is truly the last hurdle or simply a ploy. Finally, if they genuinely can't stretch their budget to your price, then go back into the discussion phase to see whether there are any elements of the deal that could be omitted to get the price down to their limit. For example, they may agree to accept the standard levels of support and warranty rather than the enhanced levels previously discussed.

Beware of negotiators trying to squeeze a last-minute concession from you by nibbling away at the deal you summarize. This could be either buying or selling. They could try to say that all along their understanding was that delivery charges were included or excluded, that insurance was in or out, and so on. Resist the temptation to cave in. Just restate the terms and explain how the deal would be changed by the new requirement they have just raised. Find out from them what this requirement is worth to them and look to see what you may have left to trade.

Before final closure, you may need to explore what each party will do in the event that problems occur during implementation of the agreed-on resolution. It's usually a lot easier to agree now on the processes for problem handling, communication, and escalation rather than struggling to do this much later, under the pressure of a real problem, when the negotiation teams have disbanded and the momentum of agreement has stalled. It is important to remember that in general a negotiated resolution is a contract and may be enforced under the law of contracts, even if it is not written down. However, the agreement may be void if it lacks consideration, was reached through duress or fraud, or is based on mutual mistakes. Therefore, if one party misrepresents the law, lies about the facts, or otherwise deliberately deceives the other party in order to gain a bargaining advantage, the agreement may be voidable.

Commitment and Documentation

Although the parties may not literally shake hands, it can be an effective tradition at the point of agreement to act as a symbol of commitment and closure. It is a powerful symbol in various cultures and will help to cement the deal. Just offering your hand can be a strong subliminal trigger to which the other party often responds automatically without thinking. This can help to overcome last-minute hesitation but can backfire if the other party feels manipulated.

Even at this late stage, the other party may feel the need to employ tricks to get one more compromise from you. Beware of them trying to withdraw a concession they had previously agreed on. They may think you are vulnerable to this tactic because to you the deal was in the bag and you may now be so anxious to conclude the negotiation that you will be willing to do so even with this last-minute change. You should pause and loop back into planning for a review of your notes from the earlier phases of the negotiation. You should return to the discussion phase to ask the other party to explain what has changed to warrant their request to withdraw a previously agreed-on element of the resolution. Read to them from your notes what they had agreed on and what it was that you had been willing to trade in return. Tell them that if they insist on withdrawing their compromise, then of course they will not obtain the benefits they would have enjoyed from your matched concession. Ideally, this will get the deal back on track to a satisfactory conclusion.

Despite summarizing what you think you've agreed, it's common for one or both parties to misremember some of the details. Therefore, confirm the deal in writing as soon as possible. Depending on the type of negotiation and value, this may be an e-mail, a letter, or a formal contract. Even when dealing with your own children, it can be useful to write down each party's commitment and post this on the fridge door!

Documentation is important, but it is only a means to an end; what is more important is the implementation of the deal and delivery of the results. Therefore, you should document the resolution only to the extent that is appropriate in order to ensure implementation. In our experience, it is better to produce a quick summary in writing followed by immediate action to begin implementation, rather than risk inaction by introducing an inordinate delay while unnecessarily detailed documentation is created.

The final step of closure is to confirm the agreement and if appropriate to sign on the dotted line. The negotiation is not over until the ink is dry and the commitment has irrevocably been made. The final stage in many negotiations is taking the binding step of legal commitment when you sign the contract or hand over the money. In a large value deal, you will have the lawyers on the team to go through the small print before signing. Avoid "standard" form contracts from the other party because these will not reflect the details of your hard-won negotiation. If the other party has agreed to produce the documentation, check it carefully to make sure it contains all the agreed-upon elements and make sure that no extra benefits or services have been added. If you agreed to document the deal, resist any temptation to correct, exaggerate, or just plain fiddle the facts. No cheating! Just let them have the agreed-upon deal. If you have rushed through any previous phases, the other party may still hesitate at this final step, but if you have closed in a professional manner, they should be pleased to sign on the dotted line.

Even with a deal that been duly signed and sealed, it may still have to be delivered. This calls for sustained commitment after the negotiation. Sometimes there is a perception by people who were not directly involved in the deal that the negotiators have let down their respective organization by agreeing to elements and timescales that they feel are unrealistic. If you are a salesperson, remember that the formula for customer delight is expectation plus one. It doesn't take much to get repeat business, but if you deliver expectation minus one, you can kiss goodbye to the next deal with that customer and to good references for other potential customers.

The challenge we would like to set is for you to leave a successful negotiation with potential concessions still remaining unspent in your pocket—and never tell the other party.

Ten Golden Rules for Successful Negotiation

The guidelines covered in this chapter identify the techniques available to control and influence events to your own advantage. They also provide a good defense against aggressive negotiators, thereby producing better agreements with fewer expensive concessions. Everyone feels they know how to negotiate, just as everyone knows how to kick a soccer ball. But try explaining the off-side rule in soccer to a beginner and compare that with understanding the subtleties of defensive negotiation. It is then that the need for clear rules becomes more important. We'll start by simply listing the ten golden rules, and then we'll explain each one in turn.

1. Don't negotiate unless you need to.
2. Never negotiate with yourself.
3. Never accept the first offer.
4. Never make the first offer if you can help it.
5. Listen more and talk less.

6.   There are no free gifts.

7.   Always isolate cost, price, and value.

8.   Watch out for the salami effect.

9.   Never make a quick deal.

10.   Never disclose your bottom line.

As you become more familiar with these rules, you will no doubt work out that they represent ten key lessons that we have learned over many years. Of course, the examples we give to demonstrate the guidelines will ideally paint a picture of us as experienced, professional negotiators, but the reality is that we have probably learned more from the painful mistakes we have made in negotiations than from the deals that went without a hitch! The examples we quote are from real deals where our clients have agreed to the essential details being used as long as their corporate identity remains confidential.

1: Don't Negotiate Unless You Need To

Always evaluate your needs honestly and buy or sell hard. If at all possible, never negotiate because it requires compromise, which comes at a price. If there is no conflict, then there is no need to negotiate. If there is a conflict but you don't need to have it resolved right away, then don't go into the nego-tiation right away. Even when there is a need to negotiate, some people are tempted to negotiate too soon. Just because the other party says that this is the negotiation phase doesn't make it so. Before you unintentionally slip into negotiation mode, remember that if you have a superior bargaining position or the other party gives you everything you want, then you should promptly close the transaction. You still have the option at some later time, if business circumstances change, to negotiate with the other party.

A good example of a problem in this area was when we discovered that one of our clients habitually included in their sales proposals a plan and timescales for the next steps, which ended with the explicit heading "The Negotiation Phase." This came to light when our client first engaged us to advise them on the sale of pneumatic components for auto trailers to a Chinese manufacturing company based in the Guangxi Province. Our client had been reasonably successful to date in selling to European manufacturers but had been having some difficulty penetrating the emerging markets in China. They asked us if we would apply our experience of negotiating in China to help them achieve their business goals. However, when we reviewed their approach, we realized that the main issue was not strictly about their negotiation techniques but rather that the standard format they were using for their sales proposals in effect turned a straightforward sale into a difficult negotiation.

We explained that their sales proposal was strong right up to the point when they indicated explicitly that they expected to negotiate—and therefore to compromise. The Chinese buyers immediately used this expectation to their advantage by performing detailed research and analysis and being well prepared to negotiate. In contrast, our client did not really expect to have to negotiate and in the past had been unprepared for the tough professionalism of the other party. We simply dropped the heading of "The Negotiation Phase" from the sales proposal and provided our client with advanced training in sales techniques with an emphasis on selling value to executive levels. The result was that our client gradually opened up that new market by selling well and never negotiating unless there was absolutely no viable alternative.

2: Never Negotiate with Yourself

People frequently try to second-guess the other party and in doing so minimize their own expectations. For example, they may ideally want to be paid $10,000 but worry that the other party may not have that much, so they ask for $10,000 or the nearest offer, hoping this sounds less aggressive. This is the start of negotiating with yourself. If you reduce your expectations from your ideal before you even see the "whites of their eyes," you will always end up with a lesser, over-compromised deal. We often see written proposals stating that this represents a first offer—in which case the buyer would be well advised to simply wait for the next offer. So, don't negotiate with yourself; work out your ideal position and don't be afraid to state it straightaway. Start with your ideal and wait for the other party to ask you to compromise. After you make an offer, wait for a response. If you jump in to fill the silence, you'll end up negotiating yourself down. Avoid the danger of assuming that silence means rejection and of making further concessions.

A practical example of the temptation to negotiate with yourself comes from a client of ours who was trying to sell information technology solutions into Egypt. The account manager had some initial discussions with the various senior managers in the Egyptian company during which the head of finance had asked for a "ballpark figure" just to help him estimate the budget projections, without which it would not be possible to even progress to the next stage of the discussions. The account manager had carefully explained that no accurate budget figures could be calculated until the precise requirements had been defined but that a sum of "around a million dollars" may be indicated. The discussions continued over several weeks, during which time the account manager and some of the key technical staff made several trips to Cairo and also ensured they had time to visit several other areas. They met with various managers from the Egyptian company and were impressed with the hospitality extended to them. Many of the discussions were about the potential impact of the political situation and the resultant economic uncertainty. The situation for the man in the street was brought home by typical tourist trips to see the pyramids, camel rides, and a journey by donkey power to other historical monuments and local markets.

Eventually all the details of the planned project were finalized. The account manager then realized that the total for hardware, software, and services would be $1.15 million, but he was convinced that the difficult economic circumstances of the Egyptian company would preclude a deal more than $1 million, so he then embarked upon a campaign of negotiating with himself and many of the key internal managers in his own company. He went to the senior executive in charge of hardware and pointed out that the buyer could purchase alternative hardware at a slightly better price from another provider in the region, and therefore the price should be discounted to that level. He talked to the senior executive in charge of software to work out what modules would be "off the shelf" and what would require some development, and he applied pressure to reduce the margins below what would normally be tolerated. He put similar pressure on the head of services, suggesting ways in which certain costs could be accounted for more imaginatively to spread them over longer time periods and so reduce the charge on this project.

It was at this point that the CEO realized they were faced with a difficult decision either to write off the substantial costs incurred so far and walk away from the deal or to sign the contract that represented no real profit for them, with the danger of slipping into a loss before the conclusion of the project. The CEO then brought us in to perform what was dubbed a "postmortem" on the deal. We were able to quickly analyze what had actually happened, as we had worked in Egypt before and knew of the difficulties that companies face when trying to enter that market for the first time or when the salespeople involved have little experience in the region.

We were able to categorize the principal problem as being our client trying to "negotiate with themselves," and we ran a couple of workshops to reinforce the correct negotiation techniques for future deals. Meanwhile, we identified several points in the contract that were still subject to some sort of negotiation, such as the number of days and level of seniority of support and whether this was to be in person in Cairo or by remote online access supplemented by videoconferencing and telephone. Hardware upgrades and software license fees for subsequent years would also be negotiated separately. We also pointed out where it was probable that variation orders would be needed to meet local conditions that were not anticipated in the standard contract. All these factors provided opportunities for the project contract to be brought gradually back into profit. Both parties are currently satisfied with the arrangements and continue to do mutually profitable business.

3: Never Accept the First Offer

There is almost always a different and better offer behind the first, so don't accept the first offer. The better offer doesn't have to be a lower price because it may be that other elements of the deal can be improved. Don't forget that the other party will be instinctively or professionally trying not to break rule 2, so they won't want to negotiate with themselves. Their opening stance will obviously be leaning toward their ideal position, probably with some room for maneuvering. Also, be aware that you can sometimes annoy the other party by accepting their first offer. If you accept too quickly, they may think they should have asked for more, resulting in their perception of a "lose-win" conclusion—they lost, you won. This may tempt them to seek retribution on you, either now or in future business.

Hollywood can provide a good example of this rule. An engineering company in Detroit that specializes in the design and construction of production lines for the auto industry was approached by a major Hollywood production company. The film required a set to be built for several scenes involving a high-tech, futuristic production line where live and robotic action would be filmed to be later integrated with computer-animated scenes. Scientists and engineers were consulted in an attempt to present a more plausible future world than usually seen in science fiction. The "artificial" production line and welding robots had to reflect this, and needed to function sufficiently well to be realistic, but clearly would not require the precision normally associated with an operational line. The Detroit company therefore felt that this contract would be easier than their normal projects and that their usual 25 percent gross profit margin would be more than adequate. The Hollywood production company opened the discussion by saying that their budget for this set was limited to $1.5 million, and after minimal discussion, the Detroit company accepted the offer. Work began almost immediately—and just as rapidly became a gigantic resource drain for Detroit. The engineers were used to being on the site to ensure functionality rather than making a series of complicated changes for artistic or aesthetic reasons! The series of changes and the unprecedented extent of travel and cost of accommodation meant that the contract was clearly going to represent a loss.

We were then engaged by the Detroit company to review their approach and to provide whatever negotiation training and mentoring was required to ensure that all subsequent deals would meet the profit targets. We began by recommending that in future the company should "stick to their knitting" by focusing on those aspects of the industry in which they were clearly a leader and avoiding the temptation of novel deals where they were outside their zone of expertise. Our analysis of the circumstances enabled us to categorize their major mistake as accepting the first offer from Hollywood. Hindsight demonstrated that the production-line scenes were critical to the movie and were commissioned rather late in the schedule that was ticking down relentlessly to release—factors that could have been used as leverage in the negotiation. But the basic research had not been done effectively, and due diligence had been rushed and superficial. As a result, Hollywood's first offer of $1.5 million was accepted when, looking back, it was clear that a much better deal could have been negotiated.

4: Never Make the First Offer If You Can Help It

If you are led to make the first offer, you are in danger of leaking your bottom line straightaway. Always ask the other party what their ideal or target price is. If you are buying, ask what the list price is. If you are selling, ask them how much their budget is, what they are paying at the moment, and what the competitive positions are. If they refuse to be drawn and insist that they asked you first, then reluctantly make the offer under protest and don't break rule 2 by negotiating with yourself. State your ideal position—your list price if you're selling or your lowest target price if you're buying.

Salespeople are often confused by this particular rule because they get mixed up between selling and negotiating. In a sales situation, there is often a list price that salespeople sometimes misinterpret as them making the first offer. But at that point, there is no negotiation underway—it is still just buying and selling. Once it is clear that there is a dispute that can be resolved by mutual compromise, then you are in a negotiation and so the rule applies not to make the first offer if you can help it.

Many buyers are reluctant to disclose their purchase budget, usually because they've been stung in the past by unscrupulous salespeople who have simply sold them up to that limit. In commercial deals, our philosophy is centered on business ethics and a principled approach to negotiation that seeks to maximize the value of the outcomes for both parties. We encourage both parties to be as open as possible with one another and to treat each other with dignity and respect so that all transactions are fair and each party can agree the result has been a "win-win." Our clients who are buyers find that they can often be successful by being more open than they might imagine, and they find that most sellers will respond in kind. They start to build trust by explaining the "ballpark" budgets and talking about their business strategy and how the respective goods or services may fit into this picture. They allow the salespeople to understand how they may be able to contribute and to see that there is a genuine mutual benefit to be obtained. If the authentic "ballpark" budget immediately rules out the goods or services on offer by the supplier, then a professional salesperson will qualify out of the running rather than risk the relationship and their reputation by selling up to a budget limit and yet failing to deliver value to the customer. We advise our clients who are suppliers to be open and honest with the buyer and to build a rapport built on dignity and fair treatment. It is important to build trust—perhaps by sharing insights into what's happening in the supplier's own business so that the buyer is more likely to open up about their organization—and their budgets.

Some of our clients feel that they should make the first offer because they have heard of research by reputable bodies indicating that in negotiations where price is the primary and overriding issue, what we would define as haggling rather than negotiating, the final agreed price is often closer to what the first mover proposes than to the price the other party has in mind. However, our view is that much academic research often necessarily simplifies negotiations to a limited set of variables and some basic interactions, while our experience in the commercial world is that most business negotiations involve many variables and elements other than just price, so we recommend that you do not make the first offer if you can help it.

An example to illustrate this principle involves an international software vendor selling to a Russian bank based in Moscow. The vendor had recently established this new business relationship and was keen to ensure that after-sales service was up to the highest standard so that additional and future contracts could be assured. During a high-level support meeting, the bank had indicated the potential for new business, as long as some current operational problems could be resolved. The software vendor had provided the list prices for the relevant new licenses. However, the senior executives at the bank had appeared to be unimpressed with these prices—but had not expanded on their position.

The software vendor was planning to make an offer of a 7.5 percent discount and, at the last minute, engaged us to check their thinking and review the negotiating position before the next step was made. Our analysis of the situation led us to conclude that it would be inappropriate for our client to make the first offer of this proposed discount. We advised our client to prioritize a couple of key actions: first to strengthen the technical support team so that the current operational problems were resolved before the next session with the bank's executives and second to dig deeper into the bank's commercial position and be confident of the underlying reason driving the bank's potential further investment in the software range. We flew into Moscow in the snowy depths of winter to assist with the research and came to the view that the two parties had not yet reached the point of negotiation and that our client should first try to focus on selling the value case. The outcome was that the bank responded with some positive signals to the business case and were particularly complementary over the support that had ensured their systems were achieving the response times and service levels necessary for their business. However, the bank came back with some demands for concessions such as a 10 percent reduction in price, better payment terms, and a permanent support presence. It was clear we were now into a negotiation, but we had not made the mistake of making the first offer. As the negotiations continued, it became clear that the bank was much more concerned about ongoing support and technical advice than it was about the price. We were able to settle on a 5 percent first-year discount for the new licenses on the understanding that this did not set a precedent, in return for guaranteeing the availability of key technical support people for the duration of the bank's expansion project. We all enjoyed a celebration in Moscow that happened to coincide with St. Patrick's Day. It was still very cold on the pub crawl, searching for Irish bars in Moscow, but there were many warming pints of Guinness with vodka chasers consumed by the American and Russian teams—and ourselves.

5: Listen More and Talk Less

We have two ears, two eyes, and one mouth—so use them in those proportions! This is the 80/20 rule. Watch and listen 80 percent of the time and use your talking muscles for only the last 20 percent. Good negotiators lead by listening, not by talking. Let the other party ramble on even if it sounds like rubbish. You must bide your time and bite your tongue. Continued silence will provide you with the opportunity to pick off their position by their leaked signals of movement. Also, don't forget that while you are listening, you can't leak your own position and give them the advantage. Your body language and eye contact will be important to reassure the other party that you are actually in receive mode. Sit up and look toward them to show that you are interested. At appropriate intervals, check that you grasp their points by summarizing to them what you think they've said, but do this to the minimum extent needed to reassure the other party you are really listening. You should be aware of the danger of simply using the time when the other party is talking to formulate your own next utterances, rather than actually absorbing what is being said to you.

A practical example of this principle comes from our experience in Ghana. We had already done some work in the country, so when one of our clients wanted to extend their presence there, they engaged us to advise on the most appropriate approach to take in the negotiations. Our client was a Dutch telecommunications company, and their relevant product was packet bandwidth specifically bundled for the financial services industry. Our client had already approached large international banks with subsidiaries in Ghana but was not making much headway. We felt that a more local drive would be better, one that took into account the traditions of the country and appealed to senior executives in the regional banks. A marketing campaign was created along those lines and generated a few good leads for the salespeople to explore, some of which progressed into negotiations.

Our advice was to put aside lots of time in the prenegotiation stage to really get to know the individuals and allow those contacts to grow into genuine personal relationships. We emphasized the importance of active listening and the willingness to open up about personal circumstances, values, beliefs, and family commitments. We advised our client to start every meeting with some "social time" when they should not expect to talk business until the other party began to move the conversation in that direction. Until then, they should patiently exchange news about the health of family members, the state of the roads, where best to eat, the heroism of the Ghanaian national soccer team, and so on. We recommended to our client that when the other party moved the topics onto business subjects, they should then feel free to join in but to plan to talk a lot less than usual and to listen a lot more. In training negotiators, we often find that buyers are better at getting the 80/20 balance right than salespeople are.

We explained that as the negotiation progressed into the discussion phase, our client should allow plenty of time for the bank's executives to describe their business and its current goals, its objectives, the strategies they were adopting, and the plans and projects they were currently pursuing. We nominated one person from our client's team to act as "observer"—a scribe to take verbatim notes, in other words, to write down exactly what was said and to pay particular attention to any negotiation signals. This proved its worth during a break in the proceedings when the observer's notes were checked to see exactly what had been said about prices. The bank's finance manager had said, "We normally expect a discount of about 10 to 15 percent for deals of this type." Our client had initially not grasped all the subtleties of this statement, and it was only when reading the verbatim notes that the wealth of signals became apparent. The bank had used the word *normally,* which could be an implied signal that the current deal may not be considered a normal type and therefore may not warrant such a big discount. Another signal was the use of the softer term *expect* rather than harder terms such as demand, insist, or require. A third signal was the choice of the word *about,* which could indicate an approximation with some room for negotiation, rather than a precise discount. The final signal was the use of a range of discount percentages (10 to 15 percent), which our client could interpret as an indication of the bank's willingness to start negotiating at 10 percent!

As the negotiation progressed, it became clear that the bank was much less focused on a few price percentage points than it was on risk management of the project, the quality of the product, and delivery by specific target dates. It was insistent that its personal and business customers must not be adversely affected by the project. Our client was therefore able to agree on a deal that traded concessions about risk, quality, and delivery for an excellent price. The lessons learned by our client were to talk less, listen more, and watch out for signals—and write down what was said.

6: There are no Free Gifts

One of the basic principles of negotiation is mutual compromise, and our very human nature seems to place a high value on reciprocity. When we are given something, we often feel obliged to give something in return, or we feel embarrassed if we are caught unprepared and therefore have nothing in hand to exchange. This sense of obligation is ingrained and practically universal across cultures. We all seem to understand the saying "You scratch my back and I'll scratch yours." So, don't be tempted to give away a free concession. Always ask for something in return. Free gifts are not always money but can be the disclosure of useful information or even giving up your time too easily, without anything in return. Nobody values a free gift for long. It immediately decreases in value once it has been offered—and a free gift today becomes tomorrow's starting point. That may not matter too much in a one-off transaction, but in an ongoing relationship, if a seller gives away a 10 percent discount on one deal without obtaining anything in return, that will set the expectation in the buyer's mind for the next deal.

This is sound advice that we give our clients in sales organizations, and one of the reasons we can be confident of its validity is that many of our clients who are buyers have told us that in the past they made use of the "gift ploy" and led suppliers into giving a free gift. They later came to realize that this tactic can backfire. For example, one company in Italy needed to secure supplies of high-grade PTFE granules for their production processes. Their policy was to source the majority of their needs from one supplier but to use a second source for the remainder so they always had current experience with an alternative supplier who could ramp up delivery if the primary contract got into difficulties. There were several potential suppliers, but only a few could guarantee the required consistency of high quality in the areas of mechanical, thermal, and electrical properties. One of these suppliers was based in the United Kingdom and was keen to expand its Mediterranean sales.

The Italian company did not treat as "strictly confidential" the names of the potential suppliers they thought could meet the stringent technical specifications. And if you were familiar with the industry, you might suspect that for some of the suppliers on the "leaked" list, it would perhaps be a difficult challenge to score highly on the tough, weighted criteria of the tender. Nevertheless, the Italian company seemed to have a few credible alternative suppliers, and this sharpened the competitive focus. At the same time, there were rumors in the industry that the Italian company may have landed a couple of new long-term contracts for their products. Against this backdrop, the U.K. supplier suggested a significant discount simply to get the business—there was no associated condition or concession. This is what we would call a *free gift*, which in this case became just the start of a downward discount spiral because each year the Italian company expected to get a bigger discount. The U.K. supplier tried to make savings to compensate for declining margins, and this created some problems with delivery, documentation, and support. In time, the problems extended to occasional quality hitches. The Italian company delayed some payments and then activated penalty clauses. The commercial relationship eventually broke down, and it was at that point we were engaged to provide negotiation training in the context of supply-chain management. It is interesting to note that although the Italian company benefitted from the "free gift" in the short term, they eventually paid the price in disruption to their supply chain and their ability to satisfy their own customers. The negotiation lesson to be learned from all this is: no free gifts.

7: Always Isolate Cost, Price, and Value

At the end of a negotiation, most people—ranging from rookie to professional—will wonder if they could have achieved a better deal. A good professional should simply shrug off any lingering doubt or regret and move on to the next challenge. But to avoid the rookie regret, don't forget the essential differences between cost, price, and value.

- Cost is how much a concession will cost you.
- Price is how much you want to charge for it.
- Value is what it is worth to the other party.

For example, the cost of a washer for a sink tap may be 10 cents. The price to remove an old leaking washer and fit a new one may be 15 minutes of your time, say $20. The value to the other party is that the leak doesn't ruin their bathroom floor and destroy the living room ceiling plaster at a $1,000 replacement. A good negotiator will avoid confusing cost, price, and value and will separate each of these concepts while analyzing each one in isolation, before creatively planning how best to join them together to achieve a "win-win" deal to the advantage of both parties.

You may be able to aim for a "super-win" where both parties get high-value concessions at low cost. For example, you may agree to finish the job early, before the family celebration starts, if they pay 100 percent up front in cash. You should invest time and effort on each negotiable element of the deal that you are willing to trade and ask yourself the three trading questions covered earlier: what's it going to cost me, what's it worth to the other party, and what do I want in return? These three questions will help you to evaluate both sides so that you can understand what could possibly be traded. Rookies and poor negotiators focus primarily on the price. Good negotiators know that there may be dozens or even hundreds of negotiable elements in a deal, and for each of these they isolate cost, price, and value and consider each in turn.

For example, one element of the deal may cost you $1,000 to give away but may represent a value of $5,000 to the other party. This is what we call a lever. Of course, what you want in return is something worth at least $5,000 to you—and wouldn't it be a good "super-win" if the cost of this to the other party was only $1,000? The trick to achieving this is to avoid confusing cost, price, and value; to separate each of these concepts while you consider each one in isolation; and then to join them together in an imaginative deal. This can create additional value, just like the alchemist's approach—first separate and then join.

A practical example of this principle comes from our experience with three companies trading together across the United States, Holland, and the United Kingdom. The U.S. company was creating strong, heat-resistant aromatic poly-amide fiber products used in applications ranging from aerospace to military to bicycle tires. The fiber products were to be packaged and distributed by a Dutch subsidiary to a company in the northern United Kingdom that was manufacturing ballistic-rated body armor. This company engaged us to review and improve their negotiation techniques after they had some serious problems with this otherwise lucrative supply contract.

Our analysis revealed that our U.K. client had not properly separated cost, price, and value and had failed to grasp the critical importance to the Dutch distributer of them always hitting a particular delivery window. The product was being shipped by container across the North Sea from Holland to the United Kingdom's East Coast and then by road across the Pennine Hills. The maximum number of hours that the truck drivers could legally work was nine hours each day (with a 45-minute break) extended twice a week to ten hours, giving a weekly maximum of 56 hours. The shipping schedule was tight, and the distributor's best price had been possible only by them assuming that all deliveries, unloading, and inspection would run like clockwork so there would be no need for three or four expensive overnight stops for the truck drivers each week. This had not been understood by our client, who had other operational logistics to consider as a higher priority. This meant that the truck drivers often reached the maximum driving time and were legally obliged to stop work. This incurred immediate costs and could result in further shipping schedules being missed. In some weeks the operation ran smoothly, while other weeks were filled with problems, arguments, and customer complaints. The result was that the distributor wanted to pass all the additional costs onto our client.

There was an added irony in the situation because our client was finding problems caused by the distributor using single-ply transport bags for the product, which often resulted in damage and costs that could have been avoided had the contract specified the use of three-ply bags. It seems that both parties to the negotiation had failed to fully grasp all aspects of cost, price, and value in the deal. We instigated a series of meetings with all the stakeholders that developed into a renegotiation of the contract that took into account all the relevant elements. This encouraged all parties to openly declare their critical interests and allowed options to be evaluated. Eventually, when each party felt they understood enough about the other's costs and values, they were able to price and trade mutual compromises to the benefit of all parties. The negotiating lesson is to do your research so you can isolate cost, price, and value.

8: Watch Out for the Salami Effect

Don't itemize every element of the deal and price them individually. Start with a complete value-oriented price, such as $1,000 in total for materials, labor, cleanup, and a five-year guarantee. Don't offer the details of $300 on materials, $500 for labor, $100 to clean up, and $100 for a five-year guarantee. The other party may know where to buy cheaper materials and then query your labor rates, saying they'll do the cleanup themselves and forego the guarantee—thank you very much! So, a $1,000 deal easily becomes a smaller job with $200 in materials and $400 in labor. That's the salami effect.

Of course, if you are a sales organization, you will have spent a great deal of time and effort making sure that you know exactly how much every component of your product or service costs you. But this is business-critical data and should not be revealed to anyone else. You need to know all the input costs of the raw materials and energy going into your "salami" so you know how much to charge for each slice, but don't volunteer any information that may find its way to customers or competitors. You may have to reveal some of the details of your salami slices if the other party insists, but only do so when necessary and only to the minimum extent demanded. Never band your expectations—it leaks your bottom line. For example, if you, say, you are looking for a 10 to 15 percent discount, which end of that band do you think you are more likely to get?

An example of the salami effect involves a client who engaged us to "audit" their negotiation process because they were not achieving the margins they felt were possible and desirable. The company was a technology provider, and they were about to negotiate a deal to supply extensive hardware, software, and services to the Swedish Pensions Agency. When we examined our client's processes for planning and executing a negotiation, we felt they were basically sound. The experience and skill levels of the team also appeared to be up to the job. However, when we looked at their process for creating the written documentation, such as a bid in response to a tender, we found they employed a standard that required a comprehensive "bill of materials" to be included. This had been done so that all the various internal stakeholders could sign off on every deal. This ensured that the hardware, software, and services executives could each be confident of delivering their contribution to time, cost, and quality—and still make a profit. Unfortunately, this standard document had not been restricted to internal functions but had become one of the many appendixes normally included in bids.

We were able to categorize the problem as the salami effect (although we couldn't resist renaming it for the Swedes) because they were presenting their customer with a smörgåsbord of options from which the customer could pick and choose the tasty morsels they wanted while leaving our client with an unsatisfactory, unprofitable, and unpalatable deal. We were pleased that our client immediately amended their standard so that the offending document was classified as "commercial-in-confidence, for internal use only."

However, don't just think this potential problem applies only to the bid process. Both buyers and sellers can fall into the trap of putting too much detail into their negotiation proposals in the middle of the negotiation process. The lesson to be learned from all this is: watch out for the salami effect.

9: Never Make a Quick Deal

If you are offered a quick deal, just say maybe. A quick deal usually ends up in regret. You may be dealing with an unscrupulous negotiator who knows that we tend to associate a progressively higher value with things that are more difficult for us to obtain or when we believe there is only a limited amount of time available for gaining access to the desired resource. Research has shown that scarcity in quantity or time seems to make us want something even more, and this may pressure you into a hasty decision. Therefore, slow down and check your understanding of their offer by repeating it back to them. Similarly, you may have just made a proposal to the other party and were then surprised with a sudden acceptance or counteroffer. It may be that the other party is trying to increase the tempo of the deal because they think they've spotted an advantage for them or a mistake by you that you've missed. They may not try to hold you to your mistake but are likely to want another concession from you to backtrack from your error. Give yourself time to check the proposed agreement thoroughly. Never be afraid to take a short break and review your position before concluding proceedings.

A simple example of this principle relates to an engineering client from the United Kingdom who had engaged us to provide negotiation training for their sales team. As part of our work, we acted as observers during a negotiation with a Brazilian aircraft company wanting to buy components for landing gear. The main elements of the deal were discussed, and it looked as though an agreement would be reached without too much difficulty.

During discussions about what currency would be applied, the proposals had been made in Brazilian real (BR), although some imported elements were priced in U.S. dollars. A computer model was used to handle conversion into British pounds sterling and also into U.S. dollars. There had been no problem with the conversion of currencies on the ex-works price and other charges, but when it came to agreeing on certain delivery charges, a unit figure was discussed that translated into a batch price of around BR50,000, but our client's model had been left in U.S. dollar mode. As a result, our client thought they were being offered £24,000 when in fact, because of their own conversion error, they were being offered only £15,000. The buyer moved quickly to summarize their overall offer, which was comfortably within the limits that our planning sessions had set. However, rather than rush into immediate acceptance, we asked for a recess—ostensibly to make some telephone calls and discuss the proposal. We used the time to crawl all over every element of the deal, and our client's finance expert spotted the error. This gave us the incentive to go back with a slightly amended counteroffer. The lesson to be learned is: never make a quick deal.

10: Never Disclose Your Bottom Line

Don't disclose or even discuss what your bottom line is or was. Don't reveal it before you start the negotiation, not during the discussions, and never after a successful "win-win" conclusion. Beware of falling under the spell of an adrenaline rush at the end of the negotiation and allowing yourself to disclose what your bottom line may have been. Disclosure will always give the other party an undue advantage over you. People learn their negotiation skills from their interaction with you. They also learn your limitations and abilities by postnegotiation analysis. So, don't let them know how you work under any circumstances. Keep them guessing about your no-deal positions, and they will have to move more toward you than you will toward them.

After a successful "win-win" negotiation, it sometimes happens that even the most experienced people are tempted to inflate their own role and contribution when chatting to people who were not involved in the deal. They may even exaggerate the rewards that were achieved so it sounds more like a "win-lose" against the other party. If this loose talk gets back to the other party, you may find that it sours any chance of a good future relationship and may even jeopardize the current deal if the goods, services, or payments are still in the pipeline.

Finally, if you were to reveal directly to the other party after the deal that you could have given more concessions before getting to your bottom line, you will cause the other party to feel that what they had previously perceived to be a "win-win" has suddenly deteriorated into a "lose-win" against them. You don't want that to happen because it may tempt them to seek retribution on you, either now or in future business.

A practical example of this comes from an experience that triggered a wheel manufacturer in the United States to engage us to mentor their negotiators following their deal with a Japanese car maker. Our clients had begun the deal with a tour of their facilities in the United States, and when it looked as though it was going to be successful, they agreed to hold the final negotiation sessions in Japan. Our clients planned well and had defined what their bottom line looked like on several dimensions. Their major focus was on the overall price, but there were also other important elements to get right. In Japan, the team felt a little jet-lagged but were keen to get started—and they were pleased with the progress they made toward an agreement. As the final day ended, they all shook hands on the deal, and the Japanese hosts took the American team out for dinner followed by karaoke and sake. In the relaxed atmosphere, the Japanese procurement director asked the lead American negotiator if they were happy about the deal. The American answered politely along the lines that they were in fact "very happy" with the deal. But this seemed to set off alarm bells in the Japanese camp because the night was drawn to a swift conclusion with arrangements for the negotiation to be revisited first thing the following morning. The Americans were thrown off balance because they thought the deal was done and they were booked on their return flight at midday. Nevertheless, the teams resumed early the next day, and it seemed that a few relatively minor concessions were the price the Americans had to pay for having disclosed they were a bit too happy with the outcome. Another round of handshakes followed, perhaps more tentative and with a bit more humility this time—followed by a mad dash to the airport.

Summary of the Ten Golden Rules

If you follow all the guidelines that have been discussed in this chapter, you will rarely feel the pain of the loser's regret, something often experienced by nonprofessional negotiators who fail to recognize that there are some golden rules to follow when resolving conflict.

1. Don't negotiate unless you need to.
2. Never negotiate with yourself.
3. Never accept the first offer.
4. Never make the first offer if you can help it.
5. Listen more and talk less.
6. There are no free gifts.
7. Always isolate cost, price, and value.
8. Watch out for the salami effect.
9. Never make a quick deal.
10. Never disclose your bottom line.

Negotiation Planning in Practice

As we covered earlier in the five phases of negotiation, the first and most critical phase is planning. You should also review and refine your plans during and in between all the other phases. There may be exceptions, of course, because in some types of negotiation there will be little chance of specific planning in advance such as in crisis negotiations triggered by threatened self-harm or the taking of hostages. Planning for these situations is much more generic and is an integral part of the rigorous training and skills needed by crisis negotiators. However, let's consider the example of a complex commercial negotiation for which you have sufficient time to plan. Let's assume you are not negotiating as an individual in your own right but that you represent an organization. This immediately raises the probability that each of the different stakeholders in your own organization will have divergent views about the purpose of the negotiation and how their various values, interests, and priorities can be represented. Your first task will be to consult with these internal stakeholders: agree on your terms of reference, decide the objective for the negotiation, and obtain the authority needed for you to do your job. This is often easier to do in a sales organization that has processes designed to make this work well or in a buying department that must continually source its raw materials than in a business that only occasionally needs to purchase a product or service that it requires rather infrequently.

Success in negotiation is often based on careful analysis of the other party's current and prospective circumstances. Experienced negotiators will search for positive or negative factors that the other party may not anticipate or fully appreciate. Sometimes you may see opportunities that the other party may not be able to exploit at all or not without your skills and capital. Seizing on key elements before the other party has critically analyzed them can create an advantage for you. Search for synergies with your current operations and those of your associates in your business network. Also look for such things as government grants, export credit guarantees, tax breaks, financial formulas, and so on. All these may give you an advantage as a deal is developing, and it may be worthwhile to seek specialist advice once you have done your first cycle of planning so that your second cycle may be even more informative. Of course, your advisors may also point out pitfalls that you had not spotted. Good planning will also help you to decide when and how to place elements on the negotiating table to your maximum advantage.

The planning phase does not just cater for the case when the negotiation all goes according to plan. You may find the reality is that the negotiation is derailed at every turn, and it may take all of your communications skills to get it back on track. The other party may initially be hesitant to be as cooperative as you, and they may take a stance that seems illogical. Your planning should therefore also include a search for any independent standards, objective guidelines, or rules of precedent that both parties may be able to respect and that you can use as a lever for adjusting the stance taken by the other party.

Some negotiations will simply represent "business as usual" with no profound implications for your organization. But some key negotiations may lead you into unchartered waters, and so you may already have performed a SWOT analysis before setting the goals and objectives for the negotiation. Check that you are now bringing into your detailed negotiation planning the following factors that provide the SWOT acronym:

- *Strengths*: The characteristics of your organization that should give it an advantage over others. In particular, you should consider what strengths you may be able to bring to bear in the planned negotiation.

- *Weaknesses*: The characteristics that may place your organization at a disadvantage relative to others. You should spend time considering your specific weaknesses that you hope the other party won't be able to take advantage of—and prepare yourself to defend your negotiating position to the best of your ability.

- *Opportunities*: External factors that offer you the chance to improve performance or profitability. You now need to focus on those opportunities presented by the current negotiation.

- *Threats*: External elements in the environment that may cause trouble for your organization. You will want to plan specifically for how you are going to deal with any of those threats that may be relevant to the negotiation.

If you are planning to enter into a negotiation that is taking you outside your current commercial boundaries, then you should already have analyzed several important factors before committing your organization to the venture. These factors will be political, economic, social, technological, legal, and environmental (PESTLE) issues that your organization has probably already documented. Perhaps now is the time to revisit your PESTLE analysis to check that you are bringing into your detailed negotiation planning the required dimensions of the current and anticipated situation in those areas that provide the PESTLE acronym. This type of analysis is used by many experienced negotiators, both in the domestic and international arenas, in determining the opportunities and risks presented by the negotiation.

- *Political*: Research and consider the political situation of the countries and regions relevant to your negotiation.

- *Economic*: Make sure you are up-to-date with the prevalent economic factors and consider how these may affect the industry and your negotiation.

- *Social/cultural*: Research and analyze the various social and cultural factors that may have a bearing on your negotiation. If certain social or cultural factors are important in the industry, decide how you will deal with these in the negotiation.

- *Technological*: Make sure you are up-to-date with the latest technological innovations that may be relevant to the negotiation. If anticipated changes in technology may affect the structure of the industry, then you will need to plan in detail how you are going to either include or exclude these from the negotiation.

- *Legal/regulatory:* Research and consider any current or proposed changes in the legislation that regulates the industry, and plan how you will take this into account for the negotiation.

- *Environmental/ecological:* Make sure you are fully aware of any environmental or ecological concerns that may be relevant for the industry, and build into your negotiation plan the tactics you will use to deal with any such factors.

The following chapter presents you with the RDC ten-point plan as a detailed guideline and key working paper to help you achieve a successful negotiation. We're aiming for a mutual "win-win" outcome, and we have compromise in mind. Obviously, we want to minimize the compromise we make and get the best deal for ourselves. That's what the first "win" means in the term *win-win*. To achieve this, you need to create a comprehensive and intelligent plan. But that doesn't mean iron-clad certainty. General Douglas MacArthur paraphrased a saying by Field Marshal Helmuth von Moltke that no plan survives contact with the enemy. If they couldn't create such a plan, then it's doubtful that we can either. However, that doesn't give us an excuse for failing to plan to the best of our ability.

The RDC Ten-Point Plan

There are two equally valid ways for you to read this chapter. First, you will want to read it for the first time, out of general interest, to become familiar with the concepts involved in planning a negotiation and to pick up the tips we offer on how to approach the topic. Second, once you have read the whole book and you are preparing for a real negotiation, you will want to read this chapter again as a practical step-by-step guide to completing a real ten-point plan of your own.

We are gradually going to build up a plan that will eventually look like Figure 7-1. Don't worry if you can't read every part of it here; this is just to let you see an overview of the whole plan. We are going to go through each element of the plan in some detail in the sections that follow.

1. Reason for the conflict - list the issues

2. List the interests around these issues

a) For our side	b) For the other party

3. Interests as measureable objectives (the analysis of wants and needs)

a) For our side	b) For the other party
i.e., money	
time	
people	
product, etc.	

Wants

Needs

Bottom line = no deal

4. Identify the common ground

5. Power base

Ours	Theirs
Cost to them if we reject their terms	Cost to us if we reject their terms
Cost to them if we accept their terms	Cost to us if we accept their terms

6. Information we need to obtain

10 Questions to ask:

Starting with:

1. Who
2. What
3. When
4. Where
5. How
6. Why
7.
8.
9.
10.

7. Information that we hold

a) that helps us if we disclose it.	b) that hinders us if we disclose it.

8. Our team roles

Leader
Summarizer
Observer
Others

9. Their team

Roles

Styles

Track record

10. The three trading questions (3TQ)

For each negotiable element:

1 – What's it going to cost me?
2 – What's it worth to the other party?
3 – What do I want in return?

Figure 7-1. The ten-point plan

We'll now go through each part of the planning document in Figure 7-1 in some detail, beginning with the box in the top-left corner.

Plan Point 1: What Is the Reason for the Conflict?

The negotiation could be of any type, including a disagreement with colleagues in your own organization, a simple external commercial deal, diplomatic nego-tiations, lawyers trying to settle out of court, a political party seeking to imple-ment its legislative program, hostage situations, or ransom for money. Your first step is to try to clarify the issues. In other words, what are the real reasons for the conflict. Often, there is confusion between the underlying causes of the conflict and the more immediate triggers that may have suddenly precipitated a crisis. There may also be confusion between the real underly-ing issues and the more emotional reactions and stances taken by the people affected by the conflict. Our human nature often leads us to react emotionally rather than with cold logic in a conflict, and so we get mixed up between deal-ing with the situation and dealing with the people involved in the situation.

Many conflicts arise when the counterparties hold incompatible beliefs about the way that their relationship or transaction was supposed to be conducted. Sometimes, conflicting assumptions are made by both parties at the outset, and they come to light only when things start to go wrong. Consider four main categories of relationship that can determine expectations about the way that transactions should be conducted, as follows:

- *Open market*: One party may believe they are operating under a rational legal framework of contracts, where the open market determines prices and where a supporting infrastructure of regulations and rules set expectations and limits.

- *Matching contributions*: Maybe the other party believes they have a relationship based on equal sharing of contribu-tions and matching of rewards, where inputs and outputs are all counted and measured and where any perceived cheating is a valid cause for retribution.

- *Commune*: Perhaps one party believes the relationship is more like a commune with its own "spirit" under which resources are shared without being measured and where loyalty to the commune is the highest value, but any miserly stinting on effort leads to expulsion.

- *Hierarchy*: Finally, maybe the other party believes the relationship is a hierarchy of authority, trust, or dominance that sets obligations and duties; determines entitlements to rewards; and punishes treason, mutiny, and insubordination.

These four different categories of relationship can be at the heart of conflicts if one party thinks the interactions will be conducted according to one category while the second party believes otherwise. However, let's now consider a simplified example in which the nature of the conflict is confined to more typical business interests. In the following example, we will be focusing on commercial negotiations with perhaps the easiest situation to consider: a buyer and a seller engaged in some sort of conflict. Whichever side of the negotiating table you are on, you should put aside the emotional baggage, try to forget about the personalities involved, and use Figure 7-2 to help you list the main issues that are causing the conflict.

1. Reason for the conflict - list the issues

Figure 7-2. List the issues

Perhaps it is the price. Maybe it's the timescale or delivery problems. Both sides of the table will probably be asking why it is that the other party is putting them into conflict. To simplify the example we are going to work through, let's focus on just the following few dimensions: price, specification, credit terms, and delivery date.

To start with, think about the conflict from the seller's perspective. If the issue is the price, perhaps the customer believes there are bigger discounts being offered by other suppliers; but are all the other factors comparable? Perhaps we need to better inform the buyer's perception of value, such as how much better the buyer's business goals can be met by our product or service rather than by the competition's. If the conflict is about product specification, perhaps we have been trying to sell our standard "vanilla" product, but the buyer may want some extra features included. If the problem is about credit terms, perhaps they haven't got the money available just yet. If the conflict is around delivery dates, maybe they need more time to prepare to implement our product. None of this means they're not going to buy. In most cases, if you go into a negotiation in western business, it usually means they will buy, but just not on the terms currently on the table.

Now think about the same conflict from the buyer's perspective. If the issue is the price, perhaps the seller has simply stated their list price, and there may be discounts and other incentives available. Is the seller aware of our growth forecast that will increase volumes? Do they understand our desire to secure a reliable source for the long-term? Are they aware that our new opportunities will demand better and more consistent quality? It may be that the product specification can be adjusted to meet our requirements. Perhaps the normal credit terms can be varied, in certain situations. Are the delivery dates fixed, or is there some flexibility to accommodate our needs?

Plan Point 2: What Are the Interests Around These Issues?

In the context of negotiation we all have underlying values and interests that are the core drivers of our positions and actions. We are stakeholders, and sometimes our stake motivates us to take a certain stance. The success of your negotiation will depend upon how well you understand your own interests and those of the other party. It is significant that some of our clients find it almost as difficult to articulate clearly their own interests as imagining what may be the other party's interests and priorities. Sometimes each individual may have several interests, some of which can conflict with each other. If you will be negotiating not as an individual but on behalf of an organization, this requires even more clarity of thought about divergent interests and agreement of priorities with the various internal stakeholders before you begin the external negotiation. During this planning phase, you should first identify your own interests and then consider the other party's interests. However, during the negotiation, you should try to reverse this sequence: talk about their interests before your own.

Your next step in the plan is to consider what may be the other party's interests. Your basic research should have helped you to identify some of their potential interests. However, the negotiating stance they take initially may be only loosely based on their underlying values, beliefs, and interests, and, as the negotiation proceeds, they may refine their interests and adjust their stance. Consider also the full range of stakeholders there may be within the organization of the other party; they may each have somewhat different interests. Will there be people from the finance function? Will operations be represented? Perhaps there are various technical specialists, lawyers, and so on. Build up a picture of these stakeholders and their interests.

Once the discussions have begun, you should strive to build rapport so that you can ask relevant questions and start to understand their underlying values and interests. You should pay attention both to the organizational interests that the other party will have and to the personal values and interests that the individuals may have. For example, there may be personal beliefs that are important to them or rewards such as commission, bonus, or a potential promotion that may figure in the other party's motivations. To demonstrate to the other party that you have been really listening to their interests, summarize to them what you understand from what they have told you and ask them if you have gotten it right. All this will build up your credibility in their eyes, and ideally they will begin to see you as a genuine person rather than as "the opposition." This should help to prepare them for the difficult next step—for them to actually listen to you while you try your best to explain to them what your interests are in this dispute. The ability to identify divergent interests and conflicting priorities can stimulate the creative process to generate workable proposals and eventually result in an agreed-upon resolution.

All this will be part of your plan for the way the negotiation should proceed, but first you have to make some notes to help you define your own interests in relation to the reason for the conflict—your interests around each issue. Then you should try to put yourself into the position of the other party and consider what their interests may be in relation to the reason for the conflict—their interests around each issue. Use Figure 7-3 to help you make a list of the interests around the conflict.

2. List the interests around these issues	
a) For our side	b) For the other party

Figure 7-3. List the interests around the issues

If you're selling, your obvious interest in relation to the price is that you want the highest price possible. You may be tied to your list prices, or you may have some interests around a certain volume of sales that may enable the price to be adjusted accordingly. If you are buying, it's fairly obvious that most people will want the lowest price possible. However, you may have parallel interests about obtaining higher-quality, reliability, scalability, or serviceability of the product in the longer term. If you're giving credit terms as a salesperson, you would no doubt prefer to have cash with the order. If you're buying, maybe you want 90 days credit; perhaps you have in interest in breaking into new markets and need the cooperation of the supplier to achieve this. If the issue is about delivery, is your delivery time geared toward a product that you haven't made yet, or do you have it on the shelf and would like to shift it this afternoon? From the buyer's perspective, perhaps you have an interest in coordinating delivery times to tie in with a shipping schedule for an expansion overseas.

Plan Point 3: Analysis of Wants and Needs

At this point you have to define for yourself exactly what you want to achieve from this deal and how far you might be willing to be pushed on each one of its elements. To do this, you should also consider what the other party might want. Use Figure 7-4 to help you record wants and needs for your organization and for the other party.

3. Interests as measureable objectives (the analysis of wants and needs)	
a) For our side	b) For the other party
i.e., money	
time	
people	
product, etc.	
Bottom line = no deal	

Figure 7-4. Record the wants and needs

In the example to follow, we'll simplify the dimensions of the deal to just price, specification, credit terms, and delivery date. You should set specific measureable objectives for each of these elements. Once you've documented what you want, then you can establish what you need. So, let's say we want to sell product A. The list price is $1,000, and, obeying golden rule 2, we're not going to negotiate with ourselves, so we're going to start with our list price. This is our off-the-shelf, vanilla product that's ready to roll. The next element is our credit terms. Now because we haven't dealt with this client often or because we just want the cash flow, we're going to ask for cash with the order. Finally, we want to deliver before the end of our business quarter on March 31. So, in summary, we want $1,000 for product A off the shelf, cash with the order, delivered and invoiced before March 31. That's what we're aiming for; that's our perfect world. That's what we want.

Now, in line with the planning approach of MacArthur and von Moltke, we need to determine what our flexibility may be. The other party may not like our list price. We're going to make some informed assumptions about what they may want, but before we can even start talking to them, we have to define a position for ourselves that sets out how far we would be willing to get pushed down from our list price. Let's say we would go as low as a 25 percent discount if all the other elements of the deal were favorable. We would be willing to accept a price of $750.

If that's our vanilla product A, how many additional features (bells and whistles/ buttons and bows) are we prepared to put on this to make it more acceptable to the customer? Let's say we would go as far as product A++ to make it a more attractive deal.

Regarding credit terms, if we can get the right credit check and if it's the right customer, we would relax our desire for cash with the order and go to our standard industry terms of 30 days of credit.

Finally, we would ideally like to conclude the deal before the end of this quarter on March 31. However, if we can get it done by the end of the financial year, that would be acceptable, as long as we can "revenue-recognize" the transaction this year. This gives us a lot of room for maneuver, and it's not our preferred state; that's why we call it our bottom line. But we could wait until December 31 for the right deal here. Any later than that, and we would feel as though we hadn't got a good deal.

Of course, we won't be telling the other party any of our needs, but we will be clearly communicating our wants. Let's fill in these details of the plan so we can see the shape of this potential deal, as shown in Figure 7-5.

3. Interests as measureable objectives (the analysis of wants and needs)	
a) For our side	b) For the other party
$1,000	
Product A	
Cash with order	
Delivery March 31	
$750	
Product A++	
30 Days credit	
Delivery Dec 31	
Bottom line = no deal	

Figure 7-5. Example wants and needs

At the bottom of this table is a crucial line. This is our bottom line. After this, there can be no deal. But it is crucial to understand that our bottom line is not simply about price. It is a mixed basket of factors including price. All the elements that go into making up our deal are part of evaluating our bottom line, and there will be some flexibility between the various factors so that we can afford to accept a compromise on one element as long as this is balanced out by a negotiated concession on another.

So, having established what we want and what our bottom line is, then we have to consider what the other party might want. When we get to plan point 6, you will see how to prepare the right questions you will need to ask the other party. A good way to find out what they want is simply to ask. For now, you may have to make some assumptions in your early planning, but make sure you test your assumptions as soon as possible. For now let's work on the premise that your initial research leads you to believe that they want to pay only $650, and ideally they are looking for product A++++, which has many more additional features, bells and whistles, and buttons and bows. Perhaps they want to pay on normal credit terms for the industry, which may be 30 days. Then as far as delivery is concerned, perhaps their project doesn't start until June, so ideally they want delivery by June 30. Let's fill in these details on the plan so we can see the shape of this potential deal, as shown in Figure 7-6.

3. Interests as measureable objectives (the analysis of wants and needs)	
a) For our side	**b) For the other party**
$1,000	$650
Product A	Product A++++
Cash with order	30 Days credit
Delivery March 31	Delivery June 30
$750	
Product A++	
30 Days credit	
Delivery Dec 31	

Figure 7-6. Analysis of wants and needs

At first glance at the rows in the top half of the table, it looks like in every one of these elements we have a substantial gap between the wants of both parties. However, when we look down to the bottom half of the table, at our needs, we've got some room to maneuver before we get to our bottom line. We can give them a better price, we can give them a better product, we can give them exactly the credit terms they're looking for, and we can wait until their project date. As far as this potential deal is concerned, the areas of conflict might just be centered on the price and the specification of the product.

Of course, there is one quarter of the table still blank, at the bottom right of Figure 7-6. Just as we will not be telling the other party what our bottom line needs are, neither will they be telling us. Even after we close a deal, this could still be unknown. We won't know what their ideal position may have been, but they would probably have been willing to move away from their perfect world, just as we were. When we cover how to create the "jellyfish," you will see how you take the wants and needs analysis and use it in a good proposing technique.

Maslow's Hierarchy of Needs

Setting aside for the moment our specific example of a commercial negotiation, we can now discuss other types of negotiation where you may have to try to explore the needs of the other party. In this respect, it may be informative to review the work done over half a century ago by Abraham Maslow. He identified five layers of needs in a complex pattern of human motivations: physiological, safety, belonging and love, esteem, and self-actualization. Maslow believed that the most basic levels of needs must first be met before we are able to focus our motivation on the higher-level needs. Before the basic needs are met, the individual will feel anxious and tense and unable to strongly desire any higher-level needs because their motivation is dominated by their basic needs. But once the basic needs have been met, a person may then be free to be motivated toward the higher needs.

- *Physiological needs*: These are the physical requirements for human survival. Many negotiators in the fields of diplomacy, aid distribution, and charities are all too familiar with the impact on individuals when they can't get sufficient water, food, clothing, shelter, and so on.

- *Safety needs*: These may simply be the need for physical safety, perhaps brought into sharp focus because of wars or natural disasters. In addition, there is a need for economic safety, perhaps in the form of job security. Negotiators in the areas of peace-making, industrial disputes, grievance procedures, and social services will be familiar with the issues and motivations around health and safety needs.

- *Belonging and love:* The third level of need is about interpersonal relationships and feelings of belongingness. Children are particularly vulnerable as their need for belonging can dominate their need for safety and is sometimes exploited in abusive relationships. In adults the need for belonging can drive an attachment to peers such as in gangs, religions, sports teams, clubs, and professional bodies. Negotiators often see "the other party" clinging irrationally to an untenable position because membership of their peer group requires commitment to that position, regardless of the logic of the situation.

- *Esteem:* We want to be valued by others; we have a need to feel respected, including our own self-esteem. This can often be a strong motivation in negotiations that are conducted in the public eye and where some people may look for recognition rather than a resolution. These negotiators may be "playing to the gallery" in the sense that they attach more importance to the way they act in the negotiation than in the actual outcome.

- *Self-actualization:* Maslow described this level as the desire to accomplish everything that one can, to become the most that one can be. To be fully focused on this level of need, an individual must be completely satisfied with the lower levels of need. In one person, self-actualization may be expressed in sport and athletics or in art and music; in another it may be about their professional, political, or business achievements. This can be a powerful motivation for some negotiators.

Plan Point 4: Recognition of Common Ground

In most conflicts, positions are often not quite as fundamentally opposed as they may first appear. Even when it seems initially that a conflict is huge and the different parties have wildly competing interests, a landscape may slowly come into focus that indicates there is some common ground to be explored. At certain key points in the negotiation, you will find it useful to have spent some of your planning time trying to identify what that common ground might look like. In particular, you may reach a point in the negotiation when progress appears to have stalled, and you can often get the momentum going again by summarizing the common ground and restating the benefits that both parties can anticipate by resolving the conflict.

In our example, what do we already agree on with the other party? As an absolute minimum, we already agree on three things. First, the customer wants to buy some version of product A. Second, they want to buy it sometime this year. Third, they will pay some price. Now that doesn't mean to say we're not in conflict, but when we apply the mantras of cooperation and pragmatism, quite often the common ground helps us to develop the rapport we need for a good "win-win" outcome from the negotiation. As long as we identify the common ground that the customer likes some version of product A, even if they say they want product A++++, this doesn't mean we have to move into competitive mode. We can still be cooperative and pragmatic, and we can build on this with rapport.

What other possibilities are there for common ground? Your initial research may have indicated some areas for you to explore in your questioning. We've already touched on some potential issues such as quality, reliability, scalability, and serviceability; breaking into new markets; and coordinating delivery times to tie in with a shipping schedule for an expansion overseas. Perhaps by the second cycle of planning, your initial discussion will have enabled you to revise plan point 4 to include new common ground that you have identified and that you will then write into the revised plan. This will help you during the next phase of discussion, when you can summarize the new common ground before progressing the negotiation. Use Figure 7-7 to record your initial views about the potential common ground.

4. Identify the common ground

Figure 7-7. Fill in common ground

Another dimension to the idea of sharing common ground with the other party is the concept of sharing similarities of attitudes, values, and beliefs. Research indicates that a person sending a message has a greater probability of positively influencing the other party's attitude when the receiver sees the sender as more similar than dissimilar to themselves. People who perceive others as being similar to themselves often also believe those people are sympathetic and share some common ground. For this reason, many negotiators will do the necessary research and then ask background questions to encourage the other party to share their experiences and will look for opportunities to develop the idea of similarity, mutual interdependence, and common ground. Another tactic may be to point out or even create an external "third-party" enemy to make it seem that the two negotiating parties have something more in common.

Common ground may also take the form of some relevant independent standards, objective guidelines, or rules of precedent that both parties may be able to respect. For example, one of our U.K. clients wanted to negotiate the purchase of the complete credit card "book" from a large bank in the United States. Our client wanted access to the significant numbers of high-spending credit card customers with whom they hoped to build a lifetime relationship and cross-sell other profitable financial products. They also wanted the well-known brand name associated with the credit card. Our client had calculated that they would be able to operate the credit card at lower costs through economies of scale by integrating its processing with their existing large operation. They also knew that their own debt prevention and collection service had one of the best records in the industry and would be able to get better control over defaults. But they did not want to be landed with too many old, high-risk debts that may be languishing on the books—and they did not want to pay the full asking price for the deal.

The negotiation had stalled because the bank managers in the United States was sticking to their initial target price. To try to get the negotiation moving again, we managed to gain agreement to the release of more detailed statistical information about the level of debts on the books in various age categories. There were some differences in presentation and interpretation of these figures between the United Kingdom and United States. An associate in one of the international networks of firms providing professional services in accountancy and business consultancy was able to identify a couple of useful factors. One was a conversion model to ensure that the information from the United States could be aligned with the way the U.K. bank needed to analyze the data. The other was a set of figures about the prices paid in recent years for debt of this type across the same age and demographic profiles. We presented this new basis for objectively evaluating the debt, together with a restatement of the common ground: that both parties wanted the sale to go ahead, both wanted it concluded rapidly, and both wanted to be able to tell their shareholders that they had struck a fair deal at a price that would present "no surprise" to the markets. After much discussion, it was agreed that the independent standards and precedents could be used as a yardstick in the current negotiation. Rather than have the two parties arguing about their different subjective positions, they were able to identify some common ground and then use this as a foundation for adjusting certain prices—some up and some down—in return for other compromises on both sides that then led to a satisfactory deal.

Plan Point 5: Who Has More Power?

Power is elusive in many contexts, but particularly so in a negotiation. Often the perception of power may be as important as actual power, and in many instances the balance of power can start off as symmetrical and then gradually shift to an asymmetrical position over time. Power is therefore relational and dynamic as well as perceptual. Power can be a function of credibility, which in turn relies on expertise and reliability. Perhaps the easiest base of power to grasp is that of the law, which endows legitimate power but may sometimes be corrupted or simply subject to bluff. Some negotiators may try to give the impression of having legitimate, authoritative power when in reality they do not. Another type of power base relates to expert skill or knowledge. Here, negotiators may hold critical information and resources that give them an edge over the other party. Some negotiators may have the power of being able to give rewards; others may wield the power of being able to coerce behavior. Some people may attempt to gain power by exploiting various social variables in the situation such as cultural and language differences, religious beliefs and ideologies, local institutions, and practices. We will deal with these in Chapter 11. Some aspects of these various sources and forms of power may be emotional and qualitative, while other aspects may be easier to reduce to quantitative, financial dimensions. When applied in a commercial negotiation, relative power should be evaluated in terms of the cost of acceptance or rejection of terms, as in Figure 7-8.

5. Power base	
Ours	**Theirs**
Cost to them if we reject their terms	Cost to us if we reject their terms
Cost to them if we accept their terms	Cost to us if we accept their terms

Figure 7-8. Evaluating the power base

Figure 7-8 tries to determine whether you or the other party has more power in the negotiation or, conversely, who stands to lose most if the negotiation fails to reach a resolution of the conflict. This often has a lot to do with the balance of risk between the two parties. Consider what the potential consequences are for you and for the other party in winning or losing this deal. You also need to evaluate the alternatives that may be available both to you and to the other party. For example, if you were a buyer of telecommunications services wanting to plan a negotiation with a preferred supplier toward the end of the current contract, you would research other suppliers with similar products and also consider outsourcing. Having an alternative to agreeing on a deal with your existing supplier will increase your power in the negotiation. You can also see that it is not just absolute power that is important but also the perception of power. If the other party is convinced that you have one or more credible alternatives, they will be more inclined to cut a good deal. Try to evaluate how good or bad each of these alternatives is. Next, determine how difficult it might be for you to back out of the arrangement if conditions change, compared to how difficult it would be for the other party. Work out what will happen to you if the other party defaults on the arrangement. All these factors relate to power.

Rather than providing another example from business negotiation, let's for the moment consider a lawyer negotiating for compensation on behalf of a client. The lawyer and client should agree on a point at which they would be better off taking a chance at trial rather than accepting a negotiated settlement. To establish a realistic bargaining limit, they must try to predict the probability of receiving a favorable verdict and the most likely amount of such a verdict, together with the extra cost in going to trial. Consider the case of a plaintiff who lost a thumb in a scroll saw accident. The evidence is that there was adequate training provided and there were clear warning signs not to operate the scroll saw without the protective guard being in place. But the plaintiff had removed the guard to provide better visibility of the operation. The plaintiff alleges defective design because the guard was flimsy plastic that became quickly scratched and cracked—and was easily removed. The lawyer estimates that the best they can expect is a recovery for the plaintiff of around $150,000. But the most probable average recovery is around $74,000, and there is a 50 percent chance of a favorable verdict on the balance of liability. It would cost an extra $7,000 to go to trial. The lawyer and client would therefore set the bottom of their bargaining range at $30,000, which indicates their perception of their power going into the negotiation.

To consider another example, put yourself in the position of a plaintiff in a civil suit for $100,000 in damages. Expert opinion is that if you go to court, you'll have a 95 percent chance of winning outright, so the most probable statistical outcome is you'll receive $95,000—but of course there is a 5 percent chance of getting nothing. Together with your lawyer you are negotiating with the defendant's team when they propose a settlement of 90 percent of your claim: $90,000 on condition of no publicity. Would you reject this proposal and take the chance of losing in court? Or would you accept this substantial sum right now to avoid even the small risk of the court's decision going against you?

Most plaintiffs favor the attraction of a definite, substantial gain and are plagued by the fear of intense regret if they were to reject the proposal and then lose in court. Plaintiffs with a strong case are usually risk averse.

Now put yourself into the position of the defendant. Expert opinion is that you have a 95 percent chance of losing in court. If the plaintiff's team indicated they would settle out of court if you were to pay 90 percent of the claim, would you agree to pay the $90,000? Or would you prefer to take your chance in court?

Most defendants in that position are inclined to be risk-seeking and are prepared to gamble in court rather than accept such an unpalatable proposal. They feel they have a powerful bargaining position and should be able to leverage this in any negotiated settlement. They expect plaintiffs to settle for quite a bit less than the cold statistics may indicate as the probable outcome in court. The chances are that the plaintiff in our example will settle for less than the $90,000 we have discussed so far. Imagine yourself once again as the plaintiff—would you settle for $85,000? How about $80,000? What might your bottom line be?

Let's consider a different scenario in which a plaintiff with a flimsy case files a suit for $500,000 that both sides know is unlikely to win in court—to the extent that the claim could be labeled as frivolous. However, experience indicates that in these circumstances, plaintiffs are usually overly optimistic, and defendants are usually overly pessimistic of their respective chances of success in court. Plaintiffs will probably want to take a risk in court and may aggressively reject a proposal to settle out of court for any sum that is substantially less than their claim. In contrast, defendants are usually so worried by even the small probability of losing in court that they are likely to settle out of court for a modest amount that they can imagine is just the same as buying insurance against a bad verdict. In these circumstances, plaintiffs are likely to carry a perception of power and will probably negotiate a more generous settlement than the cold statistics may predict.

Returning to the commercial realm, Michael E. Porter of Harvard Business School developed a framework that has been used for the last 30 years to analyze the competitive position of businesses. His model can be useful to indicate the perception of power that parties may have as they go into a commercial negotiation. The backdrop is the extent to which firms either collude or compete as rivals in the industry, the availability of substitute products, the extent to which entering the market is easy and cheap, and whether there are significant entry barriers and mobility barriers to potential competitors. The factors that may influence the perceptions of negotiators are as follows:

- *Buyer power:* The extent to which consumers and clients believe they can dictate price and quality in a negotiation. Their power will be greater if there are just a few big customers such as when large supermarket chains negotiate with farmers. Similar buyer power can flow from big-volume leverage such as wielded by governments or from the easy availability of suitable alternative products for buyers willing to switch. Buyers also have more power if there is easy backward integration along the value chain and the buyers are sufficiently profitable to seem able to afford to buy out their suppliers if necessary. Buyer power may also increase when there is easy real-time access to reliable market information.

- *Supplier power:* The extent to which suppliers believe they can dictate the terms of any negotiation. Their power will be greater if there are just a few dominant suppliers and if switching costs are significant. Suppliers of high-power brands such as Champagne may wield more power in a negotiation with smaller outlets. Suppliers also have more power if there is easy forward integration along the value chain, such as when brewers are profitable and seem able to afford to buy out pubs, bars, and other outlets. Supplier power may also increase when there is fragmentation of customers, such as fuel stations in remote locations, and when there is easy access to customers perhaps via the Internet.

Another indicator of initial power in a commercial negotiation comes from a type of business analysis associated with Igor Ansoff, who was an American-Russian scientist and mathematician. His approach can give you an idea of the likely perceptions that a sales organization may have prior to engaging with either existing or new customers to offer either existing or new products. For each of these four combinations of customer and product types, there is an associated estimate of the probability of a successful sale, which in turn may be an indicator of the power balance between the seller and the buyer. The probability factors are generic guidelines based on Ansoff's work and RDC's 30 years of practical experience. Sales organizations could consider using different probability factors if they have built up their own statistics over the years to officially record the success rates relating to their specific products and markets. If there are no reliable in-house statistics or if you are reading this from a buyer's perspective, then the following probability factors can be used:

- *Existing product to existing customer:* If the aim is to sell more of an existing product to an existing customer, then the probability of winning the sale is about 50/50—one sale will be won for each that is lost.

- *New product to existing customer:* The next higher level of risk is where the negotiation aims to take a new product to an existing customer. There are two types of new product: one the buyer has not bought from anyone before or one they've not sourced from this particular supplier before. The model predicts that one sale will be won for every two that are lost—there is a one in three (33.3 percent) chance of winning this class of business.

- *Existing product to new customer:* This is where the sales organization wants to take an existing product to a new customer. This might be a new name customer, or it might be a new division of an existing account. When negotiating with a new decision-making unit, the risk increases. The model predicts that one sale will be won for every four that are lost—there is a one in five (20 percent) chance of winning this class of business.

- *New product to new customer:* This is where the sales organization enters a negotiation to take a new product to a new customer. The new product might be something the customer has never bought from anyone before, or they may have previously sourced it from a competitor. The model predicts that one sale will be won for every nine that are lost. There is only a one in ten (10 percent) chance of winning this class of business.

Clearly, these factors will influence the perception of power that the sales organization has when first entering the negotiation. Both sides of any negotiation will need to consider all the relevant power factors in order to prepare effectively for the negotiation. To summarize all of this, what follows will take you just 30 seconds to read, but it may take you the rest of your career to realize exactly how it works! It is a challenge to everyone. Power is elusive, but there is a formula that goes with it in a negotiation, as shown in Figure 7-9.

We have the power when the cost to the other party for us rejecting their terms is higher than the cost to them for us accepting their terms

They have the power when the cost to us of rejecting their terms is higher than the cost to us of accepting their terms

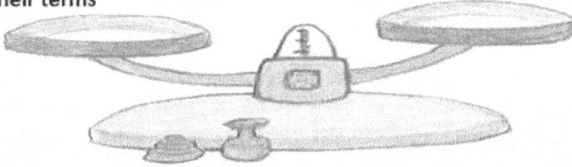

Figure 7-9. Balance of power formula

We have the power when it costs them more if we reject their terms than it costs them for us to accept. In the example we have been using in this chapter, we are selling a product for which our list price is $1,000. Let's also assume that the other party hopes to use our product in their business to generate a gross profit of $1,200. However, they feel that the margins are too tight at our list price, so they offer us a price of only $900. If we were to accept their offer, the initial cost to them would be $900. On the other hand, if we were to reject their offer, the ultimate cost to them would be the opportunity cost of $1,200 profit that they will no longer be able to realize. In these circumstances, we have the power.

Now let us consider the opposite side of the formula. The other party has the power when the cost to us of rejecting their terms is higher than the cost to us to accept. Staying with our example, let's assume that the marginal cost for us to create the product is $700 so that at our list price of $1,000 we expect to generate $300 gross profit. However, if they offer us only $900, then our gross profit falls to $200. So, the cost to us of rejecting their terms is $200 of gross profit that we won't be able to realize. On the other hand, if we were to accept their offer, our somewhat misplaced perception might be that the cost to us is the difference between the list price of $1,000 and the offered sum of $900. Our perception is an initial "cost" of $100. Don't forget our first mantra that negotiation is perceptual, not factual. In these circumstances, our impression would be that they have the power, and this perception will influence our behavior in the negotiation.

Power may also relate to real or perceived deadlines. If the other party knows you have to conclude the deal by a certain key date, you may find the balance of power shifting away from you. An example of this was one of our clients in the U.K. financial services industry with a million-dollar software agreement expiring at the end of the calendar year. Our role initially was to provide planning and support to our client. Negotiations with the preferred supplier began in October. Everybody knew that our client had to either renew the existing contract or reach an agreement with a new supplier by December 31. We felt that power was finely balanced because the other party wanted to revenue-recognize the deal in their financial year ending December 31. But there was another personal deadline that our client's lead negotiator agreed to keep secret. She was committed to a flight to take her home to her family in New York by Christmas Eve, December 24. As the complex negotiations extended to within two days of her flight, it started snowing heavily, and she was distracted and revealed her travel plans. The four team members from the other party instantly switched to a slower pace and said they had basically "cancelled Christmas." On our advice, our client's chief negotiator was told to fly home straightaway, and the CIO announced that we were taking over the lead role. We began the new round of negotiations by giving the other party the "good news" that we had managed to book four rooms for them in the local hotel, including Christmas dinner and tickets to the New Year's Eve party. However, as soon as the perceived deadline vanished, the pace picked up again, the deal was quickly finalized, and we were all home by Christmas Eve.

Power is also a factor when one party is more committed to a deal than the other. Poor negotiators sometimes irrationally escalate their commitment to an idea or to a specific monetary target that may be completely unrealistic. People who do not negotiate often sometimes stumble into high-value deals. For example, rising stars such as sports or show business personalities sometimes try to hold out for too much money in a contract only to find that their inflexibility loses them the deal. Another example we have experienced of the need to avoid irrational stubbornness is when the reputation of a show business celebrity had been taken hostage by media phone hacking. The victim's emotional reaction may be to negotiate so hard for punitive compensation that the media organization decides to go to court because they believe it will cost less than accepting an excessive claim for damages. Celebrities on the "B-list" may feel that their damages should be assessed on the scale of an A-lister, but they may find it more advantageous to listen to objective advice, accept that they are over-estimating their power in this negotiation, and agree a figure that is more realistic and achievable in an out-of-court settlement.

A similar blindness to the reality of a power-balance in a negotiation can be an over-attachment in a business to *sunk costs*—money that has been spent in the past. As these costs have already been incurred, they should be no longer relevant to the decision-making process. However, people often feel an emotional attachment to investments they may have agreed on, even though the sunk costs can have no logical role in determining future costing decisions. This includes any irrevocable commitment to future expenditure under an old contract that can't be avoided. An example of this was one of our clients who needed to negotiate with a customer who last year had spent $120,000 developing their own industrial technique that improved productivity and would have paid for itself in the next 24 months. Meanwhile, our client had invented a revolutionary new way of dealing with the process and was now offering the rights and equipment at a good price, which even the customer calculated would start to pay back within 18 months. The customer was reluctant to cut their emotional attachment to their earlier investment of $120,000 and mentioned it at every opportunity as if it were a power factor in the deal. We had to work long and hard with their production manager and finance director to convince them to write off the previous expenditure as it was a sunk cost—and to make the decision to invest in our client's new process based only on the expected payback of the new deal.

Poor negotiators seem to get emotionally locked into the pursuit of an objective even when rational facts would indicate it's time to abandon all hope. This can be seen, for example, in mergers and acquisitions, auctions, and strikes. When a protracted negotiation really gets tough, some people feel they have invested too much to quit. Such escalation of commitment can be a trap in a negotiation because it shifts the power to the other party. Their tactics may then pull you in, and their contract terms may bind you into an agreement that you will regret.

A similar effect can be seen through a power tactic you may be exposed to at some point. At the outset, the other party appears to be warm, welcoming, and enthusiastic. All their signals indicate that a good deal is probable. As the compromises are thrashed out and the detail is gradually agreed, their apparent enthusiasm seems to wane. Soon the other party appears to be cold, distracted, and withdrawn. Under the stress of anticipating a lost deal, a novice negotiator may be inclined to think they must now make more concessions in order to resuscitate the deal. A more experienced person will resist this inclination and will simply summarize the progress made so far, reaffirm what the other party is getting from the resolution, and ask if they want to deal.

Even if your planning and research leads you to conclude that the other party has more power in this deal, you may still be able to negotiate a balanced outcome. Of course, you will need to be prepared to walk away if the other party won't cooperate. However, you could begin by explaining your risk exposure to the other party and discussing the options for sharing or managing this unacceptable risk.

Think more about power and try to apply it to every deal. Who really has the power in this discussion? Exploring that question will also give you an indication as to where the mutuality lies—and maybe why the other party is coming to the table for a "win-win" at all.

Plan Point 6: Questions to Ask

You should dedicate a large proportion of the time you spend in planning defining what information you still need. In some situations there may be no chance of planning specific questions in advance, such as in crisis negotiation triggered by threatened self-harm or the taking of hostages. Professional crisis negotiators will be prepared by their training to enter these situations and listen carefully in order to absorb as much information as possible. They will be able to judge if and when it becomes possible to begin to ask careful questions. However, let us focus on the example of a commercial negotiation for which you have sufficient time to prepare the specific questions you need to ask. In your initial research, you should have uncovered some useful information about the other party, and your analysis of this data should help you to pinpoint what else you need to know. However, many people are relatively poor at planning the questions they need to ask. In plan point 3, you had to make some assumptions about what the other party may want from the negotiation. This will have been based on whatever general research has been possible, together with intelligence gathered from your network of business contacts. Now is the time to plan the detailed questions you will ask in order to find out exactly what the other party really wants. A good start is simply to ask. However, you should not simply launch in without thinking through your approach. If you ramble while you search for the right questions to ask and the right words to use, the danger is that you may give away a "free gift" of information to the other party who learns more about you than you do about them. As well as planning what questions you are going to ask, you should also plan how you will first create the necessary rapport and build the trust that is going to be needed before you can hope to obtain any sort of answers, let alone honest ones that actually give you the information you are after.

One of the problems we often see when people go into a negotiation is they don't plan to ask the right questions. This applies both to experienced negotiators and to novices or rookies. Experienced negotiators sometimes feel that they don't need to prepare in great detail because they are confident that they will be able to "wing it." However, because they don't plan even the simple questions or those that they may not like asking, they don't ask them and so they don't elicit good information. The rookies, new negotiators who don't do it often, don't know which questions to plan, so they don't plan—and it should be no surprise that the questions don't get asked and the information is not obtained.

It is strange to witness what actually goes on during the discussion when neither experienced negotiators nor rookies ask the necessary questions. Much of a poorly planned discussion centers on assumptions, theories, and gut feelings. That is not the sort of discussion that is cooperative and builds rapport. To avoid these problems, you need to plan exactly what you are going to ask. RDC recommends a minimum of ten questions, starting with who, what, when, where, how, and why. So, there's your starter for six—it's not hard to find another four if you plan for them. If you don't plan thoroughly, you'll stick with two or three questions and think that's enough. But it's not good enough—force yourself to write down in longhand at least ten questions before every negotiation. Use Figure 7-10 to help.

6. Information we need to obtain
10 Questions to ask:
Starting with:
1. Who
2. What
3. When
4. Where
5. How
6. Why
7.
8.
9.
10.

Figure 7-10. Needed information

Having constructed your list of ten questions to ask, don't simply take it into the negotiation with you, plonk it on the table, and start reading the questions out from it! Remember that we have two ears, two eyes, and one mouth, so plan to use them in those proportions. Watch and listen 80 percent of the time and use your talking muscles for only the last 20 percent. Plan to lead the conversation in the directions you have identified in your list of ten questions and then listen carefully to determine whether the answers to your questions emerge during the conversation. Don't worry if the answer to question 9 emerges before the answer to question 2. Let the discussion range back and forth until you have gathered all the information you need. You may find it useful to have ten cryptic headings in your sight to help you lead the discussion into the areas you have identified, but avoid reading your questions verbatim because this is likely to annoy the other party who may feel they are in an interrogation rather than a negotiation. When the other party is relaxed and feels that they are taking part in a genuine two-way discussion, they are more likely to open up to you. With luck, when you listen to their agenda rather than imposing your own, you may learn something really useful that wasn't on your original list of ten questions. Finally, as each answer emerges and before you lead the discussion forward, just check your understanding of that point by summarizing to the other party what you think they've said. That gives them the chance to confirm or correct your impression before you head on to another point of discussion.

Plan Point 7: Corral the Information You Have

In a negotiation, the relevancy and quality of the information you gain can often be the most critical asset you have at your disposal and a key factor in you being able to resolve the conflict and achieve a satisfactory result. People often plunge into a negotiation without reviewing and structuring the information they already have. There are two types of information you will hold before you go into a negotiation. The first is information that you hold that the other party should know. In other words, if you don't tell them this, you may not get your win. The second type is information you hold that the other party should not be told, such as what your bottom line is.

For example, perhaps you are selling a product on which the prices are due to go up at the end of next month. Should you tell them the prices are going to go up? Will it encourage them to agree a deal, or will it actually make them resentful and more likely to abandon the deal? If the information you hold was disclosed now, would it slow down this deal or hinder the win? In this deal today with the other party at the opposite side of the table, if you tell them about the price increase, will it help your case, or will they think you are trying to coerce them into doing the deal sooner, and will that make them resentful and more competitive than cooperative? Make your decision before you go into the negotiation, not at the table.

The other sort of information you hold is about any alternative courses of action you may have in the event that this negotiation does not reach a resolution that you can accept. Again, you need to decide before going into the negotiation if you should disclose this information. You may decide that your job is going to be a lot easier if they know that you have a credible alternative to dealing with them. If you are buying, you should have collected information about several potential suppliers and their product offerings. You should have checked their qualifications, credentials, trade associations, and so on. You may have been able to speak to their other customers and visited a couple that are in the most similar situation to yourself. You now need to decide whether any of this information goes on the list for disclosure or nondisclosure.

If you are in sales, you should strive to hold better information about your competition than your prospect does. If you are confident about your competitive position, you may be inclined to disclose information about your current competitors and what they are offering compared to your own products and services. As a minimum, you should be ready to disclose relevant information if the other party claims they can agree on a better deal with your competitor. You may know that your product is a better match to the buyer's requirements, your prices are more attractive, and your payment terms are more flexible. So, be prepared to defend your stance by disclosing only the right information at the right time.

If you are selling a "one-time" product, the situation may be a little different. For example, your organization may have land, buildings, or specialized equipment that it no longer requires but would be perfectly suitable for the right buyer. If you are about to enter a negotiation over such a sale, you need to decide whether you will disclose relevant information about the alternatives you have. Both parties will know that you could simply refuse to sell, but you may not want to disclose that you are desperate for cash to pay for an investment you have made elsewhere! You may be selling specialized equipment to another company that intends to refurbish it for use in their operation. If you already have a serious quote for scrap value, then it may provide a bottom line that will have to be bettered in the negotiation. Again, you need to decide what information you hold that would hinder your negotiation if you were to disclose it, what information you hold that would help your position if you were to disclose it, and, therefore, when would be the best time to release that information. Everyone on your negotiating team needs to be fully aware of what information can be disclosed and who will do this and what information must remain confidential at all times. Use Figure 7-11 to help.

7. Information that we hold:	
a) that helps us if we disclose it.	b) that hinders us if we disclose it.

Figure 7-11. Information to reveal or hold

Plan Point 8: Negotiation Team Roles

Most of the deals you do will be one-on-one. There will be you and the other party sitting at a table. In many situations, conflict arises quite spontaneously. It's not planned for, and it's difficult to understand how it's arrived, but it's there. If you are selling, the customer may not be sure about the performance that you are offering and would like a better deal. Or they feel their budget won't stretch that far and so ask for a better price. Perhaps the customer is interested but wants to postpone for six months, and you need this deal this week. Most of these negotiations will probably be spontaneous, one-on-one. However, the serious ones that you will be involved in may be critical to your career and will require a formal negotiation team. If you take the negotiation seriously, you will find that behavior breeds behavior, so the other party will probably start taking it seriously themselves. This is the point at which each party will want to build a competent and structured team.

Research has supported the intuition of many negotiators who feel it is far better to bring at least one other person from their organization to the negotiation. Such teams generally exchange more information than do individual negotiators. The collective team is usually better than an individual at evaluating the other party. Teams tend to find ways to create more value, to the benefit of both parties. However, it is critical that everyone on the team understands their role and follows certain rules designed to allow the team to function well, as covered next.

Four Team Roles

Every negotiation has a minimum of three team roles and sometimes four. You mightn't feel this instinctively, and it may not be the way you currently work, but if you don't assign at least the following three team roles, you will sacrifice some of your win every single time.

Leader

Every team needs a leader, but that label won't be obvious or even visible to the other party. You need to agree who will perform the role of leader because this person talks to the other party's leader most of the time. In a negotiation, the leader is like the orchestra conductor. They may not be the best violinist or the prima soprano, but they are the one who coordinates everyone's expertise, contribution, and timing. It's also the leader's role to bring new topics to the table. No one else in the team should be allowed to introduce new topics, just the leader. The leader is also the only person who can draw inferences from the other party's discussion, come to conclusions, and make any agreement. In fact, when we are negotiating on our own or on behalf of a client, we have a rule that only the leader can use the word *agreement*. In summary, the leader sets the pace, introduces new topics, coordinates, concludes, and reaches agreement. You should also nominate a backup leader to take over in a contingency situation. Such a situation can occur through some sort of incapacity, but you may also choose to change the lead negotiator in some rare circumstances, which we will discuss in Chapter 10.

Summarizer

The second role is a summarizer, who sits in physical proximity to the leader and works to keep the leader on track with the plan. Many leaders have a reputation for going off the planned agenda. They are said to enjoy the black runs, *off piste*, or going off on a jazz riff like Courtney Pine. You need the summarizer to bring the leader back onto the plan. The summarizer does not bring up new topics. They just recap what the leader has said. They do not draw conclusions or inferences. They repeat and summarize what the leader has said. They don't come to agreements. They merely recap the discussion points. The summarizer is there to support the leader when they go off track—or when they lose track.

Observer

The third role is an observer. This is perhaps the easiest role to sacrifice but probably the most valuable in a long-term intense negotiation. The observer is there to do just one thing—they take verbatim notes. They write down exactly what's being said. They're not there to interpret or translate or bullet point. They are there to write down what's actually said.

Consider the following example of what happens if you don't have an observer there. The other party says, "What we're looking for is a price representing about a 20 percent discount." Quite often all that's remembered by your leader and your summarizer is that someone said they need a 20 percent discount. This is where a myth of a negotiation comes in from the sometimes sketchy recollections of people who were under pressure and may have assumed certain things that later become crystallized as the myth of the negotiation rather than the reality. The leader may not hear all the signals, and the summarizer may not pick them up, so without an observer to write down the notes, you may entirely miss the critical signals.

On the other hand, if you have an observer, they should have written down all the subtleties of exactly what was said. The observer's notes will be critical later to help you realize that the other party has signaled two important aspects: that they are "looking for" (signal 1) a price of "about" (signal 2) a 20 percent discount. So, without the observer, you may have missed these two important signals. From the observer's verbatim notes, you will be able to go back and check what was really said.

In the postnegotiation planning session, someone may say, "So, they've asked for a 20 percent discount?" The leader and the summarizer say, "Yes, I heard that." But the observer can look up the notes and dispel the myth and replace it with the true facts. It could be the difference between success and failure on a big deal. It could represent 1 or 2 percent on the deal. It pays to have an observer at the table.

Supporter

Finally we sometimes have one or more "supporter" roles. In many cases, the supporter role is filled by the boss. Now be very careful. The boss, if you haven't planned for this, quite often wants to take the lead. Sometimes they are the most appropriate person to do so; sometimes they're not. Have the boss there as a supporter in a specialist role in order to have a better controlled team. Now, of course we all have the highest respect for all you bosses who are reading this, but you know it is often best for you to take a more strategic stance in many situations and let your people do their jobs that they have the right skills to perform. We agree with the line that there's no point having a dog and barking yourself.

In advance of an important upcoming negotiation, it may appear tempting for a senior executive or even the company chairperson to accept an invitation from the other party to visit their facilities to smooth the way for the negotiation. In our experience, it is best to decline the invitation, especially if it involves an overseas trip. The danger is that the other party can muster all their resources to impress your isolated boss with their charm, hospitality, and potential for profit. The boss will return full of good impressions of an easy negotiation to come. Later, when you report little progress, falling potential profits, and irrational or stubborn positions being held by the other party, the boss will suspect it's all your fault rather than clever tactics from "those nice people."

Summary of Roles

In summary, the leader is the person who knows what's going on in the deal and they've done the planning. The summarizer works with the leader to keep them on track. The observer is there to record exactly what's being said. The supporter, boss, technical specialist, lawyer, programmer, and any other people are there to be pulled in for specialist roles at the right time. Finally, it is no good having a plan for the shape of your team if there is uncertainty and confusion about exactly what is meant by the roles or who is performing what role in the specific negotiation in question. Make sure everybody in the team is committed to the assignment of roles and knows exactly what is required of them. Use Figure 7-12 to write down, communicate, and agree on the names and roles of the people in your team.

8. Our team roles
Leader
Summariser
Observer
Others

Figure 7-12. Fill in team roles

Plan Point 9: The Other Party's Team Roles

If the other party is professional, they will come to the negotiation with a similar team structure: a leader, a summarizer, an observer, and maybe a whole array of technical specialists. But they won't introduce themselves as the leader or summarizer. For example, they will say, "I am Alan, the managing director. This is my colleague, Omar, who is our technical support manager, and this is Jane, who is here simply to identify the financial part of the deal." However, it's not their job title or announced function that tells you what their role is in the negotiation. It's how they act that is important.

You also need to establish who are the key stakeholders in the other party and that everyone who is authorized to make the final decision is actually taking part in the negotiation. Beware of having lengthy discussions and agreeing to compromises on a range of elements only to be told right at the end that there is another person who needs to agree on the deal that you believed was in the bag. If you are buying, you may be told that you have insisted on such an unusually good deal that the vice president of sales has to approve it. If you are selling, you may be told that a head-office technical procurement division has to sign off on the order. Perhaps there is a parent company in the United States or China that has to "rubber-stamp" the agreement. This gives the other party, in the guise of the new authority figure, the opportunity to try to wring another set of concessions from you. So, do your research and ask the right questions to test the authority of the other party's team.

Try to find out as much as possible about the individuals you will be negotiating with. Perhaps you can find out their negotiating style and something about their background and interests. Will there be people from the finance function? Will operations be represented? Perhaps there are one or two technical specialists or lawyers and so on. Build a picture of these stakeholders and their interests.

Style

You should also consider what style the other party is likely to adopt. Don't be over-analytical, but you need to be thinking about their style and how you plan to respond. Appendix A summarizes three negotiating styles from *Getting to Yes, Negotiating Agreement Without Giving In* (Penguin Books, 1991). These styles are hard, soft, and principled. A *hard* style is adversarial, demanding, and insistent. A *soft* style is friendly, yielding, and concessionary. A *principled* style explores interests, invents options for mutual gain, and seeks a wise outcome reached efficiently and amicably.

Other research indicates that we all have strong preferences for a set of styles, and these will change over time. The styles we choose to employ in a negotiation will depend on the context and the interaction of the other party. You may be faced with a mosaic, or jigsaw puzzle, of different styles from the other party's team and should therefore be prepared to select from a range of styles depending on the type of jigsaw picture you are presented with. The main scales to consider are the degree of cooperation and the degree of assertiveness, as shown in Figure 7-13.

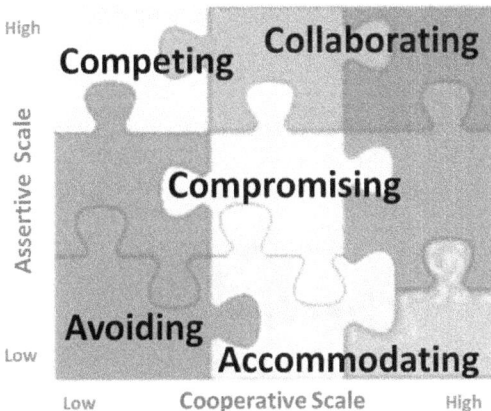

Figure 7-13. Negotiation styles

The five styles are summarized here, based on *Bargaining for Advantage* (Penguin Books, 2006):

- *Accommodating*: These people want to maintain personal relationships and solve the other party's problems. They are sensitive to the emotional states, body language, and verbal signals of the other party. They can feel taken advantage of in situations when the other party places little emphasis on the relationship.

- *Avoiding*: These people don't like to negotiate and don't do it unless necessary. They tend to defer and dodge confrontations but can be perceived as tactful and diplomatic.

- *Collaborating*: These people enjoy negotiations that involve solving tough problems in creative ways. They are good at understanding the concerns and interests of the other parties. They can, however, create problems by making negotiations more complex.

- *Competing*: These people enjoy negotiations because they present an opportunity to win something. They have strong instincts for all aspects of negotiating and are often strategic. Because their style can dominate the bargaining process, they often neglect the importance of relationships.

- *Compromising*: These people are eager to close the deal by doing what is fair and equal for all parties involved. They can be useful when there is limited time to complete the deal but often rush the negotiation and make concessions too quickly.

Dealing with Their Emotions

In an earlier chapter we discussed how your own emotions can influence your performance in a negotiation. Now is the time to plan how you can take into account the emotions of the people in the other party's negotiating team. In the initial stages you should plan to find opportunities to put the other party at ease as much as possible. In our experience, there are few occasions when it can be advantageous for you to try to manipulate the other party by displaying or feigning your own emotions. You will be much more likely to achieve a "win-win" result by encouraging the other party to feel relaxed and open. Plan to listen and watch carefully as the negotiation progresses so that you become aware of the other party's emotional state. They may display signs of embarrassment when you ask questions about information they don't want to reveal in case it undermines their position. They may display other emotional cues that can give you information about their underlying interests and their point of resistance. If a person has been calm and unemotional but then begins to show signs of agitation or even anger, it may indicate that you are coming close to their point of resistance. If the other party begins to display a sudden increase in energy and animation, it may indicate that you have begun to probe what is really important to them in this negotiation. You should also be aware that it is possible for you to unconsciously register an emotional state in the other party and for you to begin to feel the same emotion in yourself. If they are tense and anxious, you may pick this up and feel similar emotions, so plan to stay aware of your own emotions as well as those in the other party.

Tactics

Occasionally, you may have to deal with a team that feels the need to use gamesmanship to try to gain an advantage. They may be tempted to employ tricks and manipulation in their anxiety for a win. One tactic is for them to assign the stereotypical roles of "good cop" and "bad cop." One will appear to be personally accommodating, professionally collaborative, and willing to compromise. The second will appear to be adopting behavior from the other end of the scale: personally uncompromising and professionally competitive. The first person may offer concessions to see how you value these and what you are willing to give in return. The second person tries to snap up all your compromises while refusing to honor the full exchange. Your defense against such tactics is to stay professional and summarize frequently to the "bad cop" the elements "they" have indicated they would be willing to compromise on, in return for concessions you are willing to make.

Another tactic to look out for is when the other party elects to replace their lead negotiator at a late phase in the deal. The danger is that this throws you off balance and gives them the opportunity to renege on elements already agreed on by the previous lead negotiator. You may have to start all over again if the other party can't be persuaded to honor the compromises already committed.

Track Record

Then finally, what is the other party's perception of their track record with you? Many negotiations will be part of a long-term relationship rather than a one-off. You may be doing this as part of an account management review whether you're buying or selling. How well do they think they are doing in this relationship? Do they come from the position of a perceived "lose-win"? The last time you negotiated, did they lose, and did you win? The time before, did you win, and did they lose? The time before that, did you have to go to arbitration? All of this affects how the other party will work with you, and that has an impact on how you plan your team. Use Figure 7-14 to help with your plans.

9. Their team
Roles
Styles
Track record

Figure 7-14. Fill in their team

Plan Point 10: The Three Trading Questions

The last part of the ten RDC plan points is the three trading questions (3TQ) we touched on earlier. During the discussion phase of the negotiation you will probe what the other party really wants. In the propose phase, you will tentatively explore what they might be willing to exchange and how they value the concessions you may be willing to make. To prepare for this, you should invest time and effort considering each negotiable element of the deal that you are willing to trade and then, for each of these elements, ask yourself: what's it going to cost me, what's it worth to the other party, and what do I want in return?

This will help you to value both sides so that you can understand what could possibly be traded. Rookies and poor negotiators focus primarily on the price. Good negotiators know that there may be dozens or even hundreds of negotiable elements in a deal: quantity, specification, credit terms, currency, delivery schedules, decommissioning, training, maintenance, support, access to resources, research and development, key staff, warranty, liability, licenses, royalties, and many more. For each of these elements, experienced negotiators will isolate cost, price, and value and consider each in turn.

Perhaps the most difficult of the three trading questions is "What's it worth to the other party?" This requires empathy on our part to try to work out how the other party may think about and value the worth of something we are willing to trade. The economist and Nobel Prize winner Harry Markowitz concluded that investors are motivated more by incremental changes to their wealth than by the overall size of their wealth. So, if you are negotiating with a person or organization with plenty of money, don't think they will not negotiate as hard as ones with very little! They will all be focused on the marginal change at stake in the deal, and they will evaluate your proposal on that basis.

Research also shows that most people are more highly motivated to avoid losses of a certain value than they are to obtain gains of the same amount. In other words, we are generally loss-averse, but it's not quite as simple as that. In some cases, being loss-averse is the same as being risk-averse. This may be a result of our evolutionary history because predators who value threats more highly than they value opportunities have a better chance to survive and reproduce. A person who highly values an opportunity to hunt a herd of buffalo may pursue them recklessly and stands a greater chance of injury or death than a person who values the associated threats more highly. But if the hunters are trying to survive a severe drought and the only prey is the herd of buffalo, then the hunter who risks his life may just gain the advantage. The point is that our evaluation of risks, losses, and gains will depend on the prevailing circumstances. Test your own preferences by considering a scenario in which two organizations are contemplating a deal in which one will buy equipment from the other to help to generate profits in a joint venture. If you were the buyer, which of the following two negotiation proposals would you prefer to be offered: either an immediate guaranteed discount of $9,500 or a share of expected mutual profits from the deal, calculated as a 95 percent chance of you receiving $10,000?

You probably know the saying that a bird in the hand is worth two in the bush. Most people would prefer the $9,500 in their hand rather than the potential of $10,000 in the bush. Yet in strictly statistical terms, a rational person should evaluate the two choices equally at $9,500. But of course, we're not always rational—because we are also emotional, in varying degrees.

Now consider a slightly different scenario in which the joint venture has sadly failed and you are now negotiating how to wind down the enterprise. Which of the following two negotiation proposals would you prefer to be offered: either you have an immediate loss of $9,500, which you can pay now to walk away, or you stay in the venture while its assets are sold and its liabilities are discharged, with the likelihood that your contribution to the net loss will be estimated at a 95 percent chance of you losing $10,000?

Most people abhor the immediate, certain loss, and their aversion motivates them to take a risk and hope that their eventual loss will not be as much as estimated. Consider also that when people face a low probability of a high-value loss, they are often willing to pay good money for an insurance policy to cover their potential losses even if the total amount of premiums over the years will cost them more than the probable loss. They are willing to pay for peace of mind—and that's what generates profits for the insurance company. It is interesting to note that insurance policies will often cover a certain sum of actual losses but will charge a higher premium if you want cover for an equal sum in lost profits.

Research indicates that most people generally value losses at about twice the weight that they value commensurate gains. If you make a proposal involving a concession from the other party of something they possess, they will probably unconsciously feel it is worth more to them than you think it is worth to you, and they are likely to feel its loss more intensely than you will enjoy the gain. Similarly, if you are asked to give up something you value highly, the chances are you will unconsciously inflate its worth to you, but the other party will appear to you to be unimpressed by what you feel is a significant sacrifice but they dismiss as unworthy. That is why negotiations about personal conflicts are usually much more painful and protracted than those about commercial issues. Nevertheless, in many commercial negotiations there is a blend of corporate and personal values at stake. You will need to take all this into account when you are trying to determine how the other party is likely to value what you have to trade. You also need to keep this in mind when you construct the language you intend to use when describing your proposal. If possible, reframe the language so as to avoid any connotations of loss.

An example of the problems you may find in this area relates to one of our clients, a bank that had acquired two other financial institutions over a couple of years and then wanted to unify the employment terms and conditions across the three legacy organizations and bring these in line with the competition. There were quite significant differences between salary scales, bonuses, health plans, and other entitlements such as the number of days of annual holidays. One legacy organization was felt to be parsimonious with its pay scales but overgenerous with holidays, and another was the complete opposite. The third had miserly pay and holidays at the bottom of the scales, compared to the competition, but was profligate at the top compared to the other legacy organizations.

Our client consulted us before entering negotiations with the relevant employee representatives. Our previous experience suggested that the subset of employees who would be asked to give up a few days of annual holiday, even if they were offered some more money, would find the proposal emotionally difficult to accept and would place an unrealistically high value on each day of holiday. We advised that the first change to make would be to introduce a scheme for all employees giving them the option to buy and sell up to five days of holiday entitlement each year. This was described as providing flexibility and choice to the benefit of employees and their families. The idea was to help people to get used to the concept that they could buy a few extra days of annual leave if they wanted, and, conversely, they could decide to take more money in exchange for a few days less of holiday if that suited their circumstances. A few months after that scheme was launched, we drew up a proposal for the three different legacy pay scales to be unified, leaving it up to the employee representatives to propose that existing salaries be protected, which we then linked to an agreement on a transitioning sliding pay scale plus the agreement of a new holiday entitlement table. By then, people had gotten used to the idea of putting a realistic value on annual leave and had loosened their emotional commitment to their current entitlement—the negotiation was a successful "win-win."

The lessons to be learned from all this is that people attach different values to things depending on the exact circumstances and options. Therefore, you will need to give careful consideration to how you are going to estimate how the other party may value the worth of something you are willing to trade. You need to find out as much as you can about their current circumstances and then use your empathy and imagination just as much as your browser and spreadsheet.

You should also assume that the other party will be doing their research on you and will seek to understand how you may value what they have to trade. They may try to manipulate you, perhaps with the concept of scarcity. To help you avoid certain tactics of unscrupulous negotiators, we'll point out the following relevant example. According to a Greco-Roman myth, Dionysius arrived incognita in Rome and offered nine books of prophecies to King Tarquin at a certain high price. When the king declined her proposal on the grounds that the price was exorbitant, she burned three of the books and offered the remaining six to Tarquin at the same price. He again refused, so she burned three more and repeated her negotiation proposal. Tarquin then relented and purchased the last three books at the full original price. This is a traditional example of what researchers have called the scarcity principle. It seems that our human nature associates a progressively higher value with things that are more difficult for us to obtain. When a certain resource is scarce or limited in some way, we seem to react by wanting to have it even more. Such scarcity usually relates to the quantity of the resource or goods but can also relate to the limited amount of time that we may have available for gaining access to the desired resource. This can lead some negotiators to use tactics such as postponing certain concessions, or of setting a time limit on their offer, so that the other party to the negotiation is tempted to make a hasty decision. Therefore, the three trading questions can help you in two ways: first to prepare your own negotiating proposals and second to plan how you will respond to proposals from the other party. So, decide in advance on which elements of the deal you are willing to trade and then, for each of these elements, ask yourself the following: what's it going to cost me, what's it worth to the other party, and what do I want in return? Use Figure 7-15 to help with your plans.

10. The three trading questions (3TQ)
For each negotiable element:
1 – What's it going to cost me?
2 – What's it worth to the other party?
3 – What do I want in return?

Figure 7-15. 3TQ

Is This the End of the Planning Phase?

The quick answer is no. This is not the end of the planning phase, but we have at least dealt with the first cycle of planning. As we said earlier, there are two equally valid ways for you to read this chapter. First, you can read the material for the first time, out of general interest, becoming familiar with the concepts involved in planning a negotiation and absorbing the tips we offer on how to approach the topic. Second, once you have read the whole book and you are preparing for a real negotiation, you can read this chapter again as a practical step-by-step guide to completing a real plan of your own.

If you are preparing for a real negotiation, then you should now have a completed RDC ten-point negotiation plan. You will have filled in detailed notes and figures in each of the ten boxes, and, unless you are going to negotiate all on your own, this first cycle planning aid will have been clearly communicated to each of the people in your negotiation team. At this stage, your ten-point plan is what we call the *first cycle plan*. You are now ready to move out of the first phase of negotiation and take some confident steps into the second phase—to discuss the issues with the other party.

Don't forget there are five phases in every negotiation, and you will almost always go through cycles of refined planning as you progress from one phase to the next. If you are expecting your negotiation to be simple and straight-forward, with no serious consequences if it goes wrong, then a quick plan will suffice, followed by a rapid progression through the other phases. You might do this in minutes. At the opposite extreme, you may have a critical negotiation with livelihoods, if not lives, depending on the outcome. In these circumstances, you may need several weeks or months in the planning phase, followed by a discussion phase during which you break off for extended periods to review and refine your planning. Each time you do this, your ten-point plan should be updated and recommunicated to your team. Your first cycle plan is amended and becomes your second cycle plan, and so on. Each of the subsequent phases of propose and trade may be equally extended in time if the negotiation is complex and if the consequences of a failure to reach a resolution warrant the investment of time and effort. You may need to temporarily break off negotiations with the other party at any and all phases in order to check your progress and plan how to adjust your tactics as necessary to achieve your objectives, before you can conclude with phase 5, agree and confirm, as shown in Figure 7-16.

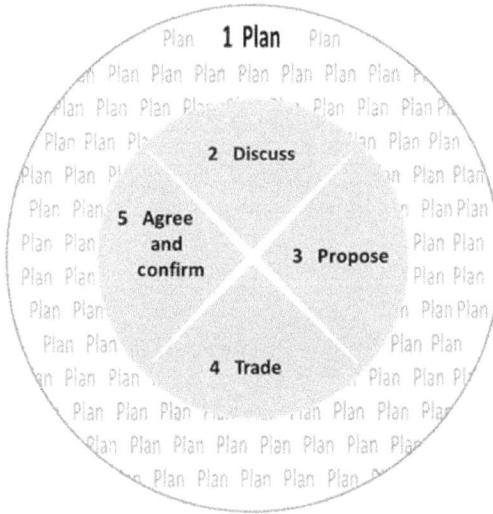

Figure 7-16. The five phases of negotiation

Negotiating for a Super-Win

We explained earlier that the RDC philosophy is centered on business ethics and a principled approach to negotiation that seeks to maximize the value of the outcomes for both parties. We have described how to build trust so that the parties can be honest about their underlying interests and seek a "win-win" resolution. Rather than locking the parties into a set of confrontational stances, this principled approach to negotiation avoids a personalized joust. It seeks a fair deal for both parties but one that they can both be motivated toward because it maximizes their own payoff. This approach can be extended to create additional value above and beyond the value that either of the parties involved in the negotiation could find in isolation—what has been called a "super-win." We have also cautioned that negotiation involves compromise and therefore should be avoided if possible in preference to straightforward buying and selling. It's now time to dig a bit deeper into these concepts and find a way of expressing the ideas so the relationship between them is clearer. Figure 8-1 shows the negotiation "bow tie" that can be used to plot the relationship between the horizontal scale, which shows the value rising from left to right, and the vertical scale, which simply indicates how the total value of the deal is shared between the parties.

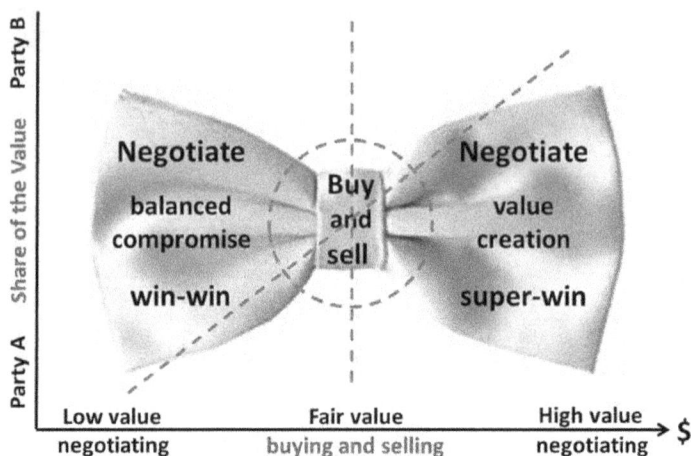

Figure 8-1. The negotiation "bow tie"

Let's begin by looking at the knot in the center of the bow tie. This represents the sort of "middle-of-the-road" deal that can be achieved through good old-fashioned buying and selling. In a fairly open and stable market, the buyers are searching for products and services that will satisfy their needs at a price they are willing to spend, and the sellers are looking for customers to buy their goods at a price that covers their costs and provides them with a living. This is a straightforward sale and purchase. No conflict and no compromise. That is the situation depicted by the knot in the center of the bow tie, where the parties in the market decide on a fair price.

To the left of the knot, we see a different situation where both parties realize there is a conflict they need to resolve. They enter a negotiation in which eventually they both make some concessions but feel that they have both shared the pain equitably; therefore, their joint perception is of a "win-win" result. However, what you see from the bow tie is that this outcome is further to the left on the scale of value than the knot in the center. It represents a balanced compromise but at a lower point of total value.

To the right of the knot, you see a much more interesting and desirable result. Both parties again realize there is a conflict they need to resolve. They enter a negotiation in which they successfully build rapport, understanding, and trust to the extent that they can be open and honest about their interests. They also look beyond the boundaries of the issues that caused the conflict, searching for other linkages and opportunities. Eventually they both realize it is possible to trade some concessions in a way that results in increased value for both parties. For example, one concession may cost party A $1,000 to give away but may represent a value of $5,000 to party B. This is what we call a *lever*. Where this turns into a "super-win" is when party B is able to offer a concession that costs them only $1,000 but is worth $5,000 to party A. In this example, the section of the golden bow tie to the right of the knot represents a total gain in value of $8,000 shared equally between the two parties. Cynics may say this sounds a bit like the magic of alchemy, which believes that base metals may be transmuted into gold. But there may be a serious lesson to be learned from alchemy, which coins the Latin maxim *solve et coagula*, meaning to separate and to join. This resonates with our approach to negotiation, where we first separate fact from perception and emotion from pragmatism before joining the parties together in understanding and cooperation, resulting in the creation of more value than either party can create in isolation.

Detailed Proposal Design (The Jellyfish)

Having worked through the RDC ten-point plan, we are now ready to go back and cover in more detail one of the most critical aspects of any negotiation: how to construct a winning proposal. During plan point 3, you analyzed your wants and needs. Figure 9-1 shows a simplified example.

3. Interests as measureable objectives (the analysis of wants and needs)	
a) For our side	b) For the other party
$1,000	$650
Product A	Product A++++
Cash with order	30 Days credit
Delivery March 31	Delivery June 30
$750	
Product A++	
30 Days credit	
Delivery Dec 31	

Figure 9-1. Example wants and needs

In this example, we now need to turn this into a proposal. We call this creating the *jellyfish* because it is multilimbed, transparent, and flexible, and if you don't use it properly, you could get stung. The jellyfish is a way of defining our perfect world for this negotiation and then identifying our outside bottom-line, "no-deal" position—what we call the *distended jellyfish*. We also use the jellyfish when we want to protect ourselves against an aggressive counter-negotiator or to provoke movement in the other party. Our objective is to keep our jellyfish as tight as possible. Our proposals need to be controlled and orderly, while remaining flexible and malleable. In the ten-point plan earlier, you identified your wants and needs in the deal. You now transfer these onto the jellyfish so that when you create your proposal, you can visualize it in its entirety. Such visualization is also a critical advantage when you are not simply negotiating as an individual in your own right but you are representing an organization. The jellyfish helps you to communicate clearly with each of the different stakeholders in your organization so they can see how their various specific values, interests, and priorities are represented. This helps you to agree on a "team" position. You can see what your perfect world is, what you want to achieve from this deal, how far you are willing to get pushed, and what your "needs" bottom line is (represented by the outside of the jellyfish). This is the limit of how far you can be stretched, represented in Figure 9-2.

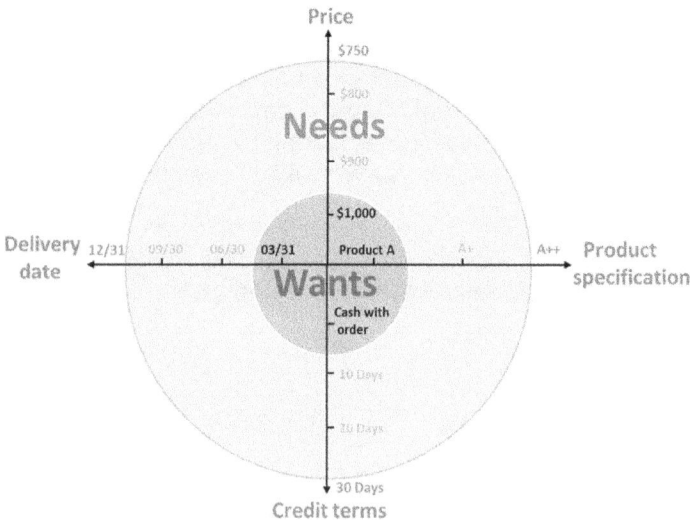

Figure 9-2. Our "wants and needs" jellyfish

In Figure 9-2, the pink core at the center of the jellyfish represents our "wants," and the outer ring represents our "needs." The right axis indicates the product specification, while the left axis shows the delivery date. The top half of the vertical axis represents the price, while the bottom half of the vertical axis indicates the credit terms.

Let's start by reading from the right axis. You can see that the product we ideally want to deliver is the vanilla, off-the-shelf product we just call product A. But if the customer wanted us to add features to this product, we would be prepared to add some bells and whistles that would take it to product A++, which would require some development.

Let's now read from the top half of the vertical axis. This shows that, ideally, we want a price of $1,000, but we would be willing to get pushed as far as our bottom line need for $750 if all other aspects of the deal were satisfactory.

Reading the bottom half of the vertical axis, you can see that regarding the credit terms, ideally we want cash with the order, but we would be willing to compromise as far as the industry standard of 30 days credit.

Now let's read from the left axis. You can see that, ideally, we want to conclude the negotiation and deliver by March 31, which helps us meet our quarterly sales target. But if the other party insisted, we would be willing to delay delivery until the end of our business year on December 31.

So, in summary, from the pink inner sector in the center of the diagram, you can see that we want to supply product A at a price of $1,000 to be paid in cash with the order, with delivery by March 31. However, from the outer ring you can see that we would be willing to compromise, if needed, as far as our bottom line of supplying product A++ at a price of $750 on 30 days credit, with delivery by December 31.

Now obviously, we don't want to settle the deal on the outside edge of every part of our jellyfish of a proposal. If we were to distend our jellyfish that far, even though it didn't leak outside of our bottom line, it would feel as though we had suffered a loss. It would feel as though we've been pushed too far. So, our goal is to try to settle as many of these elements as close to the center of the jellyfish as possible. In some deals, you may have 10, 20, or more elements to the jellyfish. There may be many different negotiable dimensions to the deal. For example, when we look at finances, there may be three variable pricing and currency structures. There may be multiphased delivery or manufacture and then delivery, which may be broken into three or four sections. The product itself may consist of five variable subproducts that can be tailored and combined into the final package.

As we're using only four elements in this simplified example, you can easily visualize what the ideal shape and size of the jellyfish should be: the central pink section. But of course the catch is that we have a conflict. The other party may not want to pay this much. They may want a better product on longer credit terms, and they may not want it delivered as early as March. Our primary task now is to settle this deal without bursting the jellyfish. Our secondary task, which will ensure we get a win out of this, is to close as many of these elements as possible as near to the center of the jellyfish as we can get them.

Using the Jellyfish to Analyze Their Offer

Another use of the jellyfish diagram can be to visually represent any counterproposal or offer from the other party. For example, after many hours of conversation and negotiation, the other party may summarize their willingness to pay $850 for product A+ to be delivered by March 31 on credit terms of 30 days. The reality is that this is our new jellyfish. We could now compare their offer to our ideal position, but after all those hours of conversation, that is unrealistic and would only tend to focus our attention back onto our wants rather than on our needs. At this stage, it would be more realistic to compare their offer to our bottom-line position. This is the position that we set ourselves in the planning phase so that we would know the lower limit of how far we would be willing to be pushed. Once again, the jellyfish provides an additional advantage when you are not simply negotiating as an individual in your own right but you are representing an organization. This time, the jellyfish portraying the offer from the other party can help us to communicate clearly with each of the different stakeholders in our organization so they can see how their various specific values, interests, and priorities are satisfied. This helps us to agree on a "team" position for the necessary compromises. Figure 9-3 can be used to help you to visualize an offer from the other party and compare it your bottom line needs.

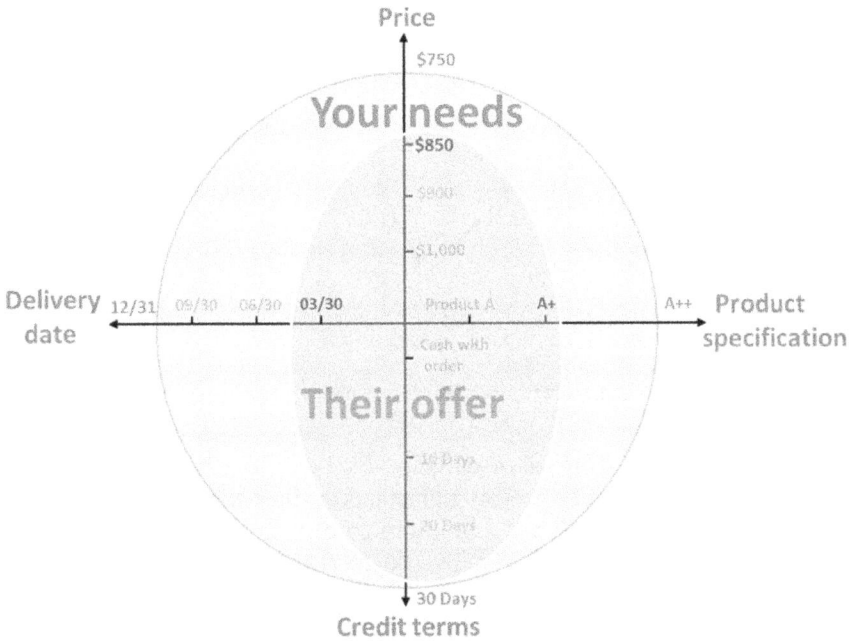

Figure 9-3. Comparing their offer to your bottom-line needs

From Figure 9-3, we can draw some key conclusions. We can compromise on a price of $850, which is a bit less than our list price of $1,000 but still above our bottom line of $750. We can agree to supply product A+, which has a few additional features over our product A but has comfortably fewer than our bottom-line product A++. The credit terms of 30 days are bit more generous than our ideal of cash with the order but acceptable even if it is right on the edge of our bottom line. The delivery date of March 31 remains well within our bottom-line deadline of December 31. The ideal obviously was our original perfect jellyfish, but it's been pulled and prodded and distended. However, it has not leaked over the outside edge. We haven't burst the jellyfish. This is a "win-win" deal.

We could make use of basic spreadsheet and charting tools to depict the data contained in our jellyfish. The result will look more professional in case you need to present it to your executives, as shown in Figure 9-4.

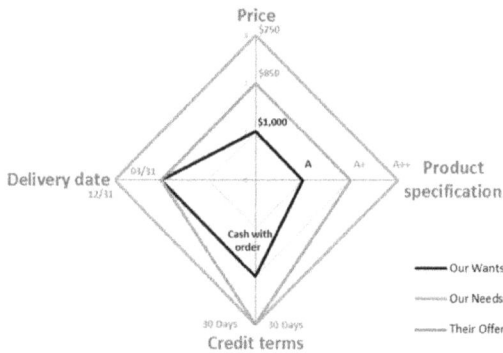

Figure 9-4. Comparing their offer to our wants and needs

In summary, the jellyfish is there to help you to plan. It helps you to understand your limitations while you're talking and enables you to make a proposal to the other party that will provoke them to provide a "win-win" resolution to the negotiation. The jellyfish helps you to communicate within your own team. It also helps you to visualize any proposal made by the other party and compare their offer to your own ideal position and to your bottom line.

Alternative Flavors of Jellyfish?

In chapter 4, we said there may be occasional situations when it is appropriate to propose two or more alternatives at the same time, so let's explore this type of situation now. One of the easiest to imagine is when a salesperson recognizes that the buyer's organization is complex, with several internal stakeholders who apparently have not yet reached consensus on competing priorities and objectives.

One of our clients had bid to design and build a communications infrastructure and structured cabling system for a U.K. bank as part of the construction of a new data processing and customer contact center on a green-field site. Our client had been given the news that, following the evaluation of a dozen tenders, they were now in a "period of exclusivity" as the preferred supplier, but with the reservation that their price would have to be reduced. The bank said it had weighted and scored all the factors and felt that our client was slightly out in front on most factors except price, which they therefore wanted to discuss. Despite several meetings, no progress had been made to finalize the contract, and yet the building work was underway, so there was a danger that decisions were being made that could be to the detriment of our client's work and would be costly to rectify.

We were asked to assist with the negotiation and started with some basic research followed by a round of discussions with the principal stakeholders. The bank's director/vice president (VP) responsible for the construction was working to a key objective tied to a cost ceiling of about $60 million and a timescale of 20 months for this project. The bank's VP for customer services had to deliver key objectives measured around quality of service and cost per customer over a five-year period. The bank's chief information officer (CIO) was working to key objectives tied to security, service availability, and head-count reductions. There was also a newly appointed supply-chain manager incentivized to cut between 10 and 20 percent off the cost of all contracts, and it was this person who constantly brought the discussion back to the need for our client to reduce the price. In our postdiscussion planning cycle, we decided to propose three options, all of which would generate roughly the same profit for our client but would present a range of designs and costs to the bank, as follows:

- *World-class flexibility*: In this we described the design and capital outlay that would minimize the lifetime operating costs and maximize the resilience, scalability, and flexibility of the systems. One key criterion was to minimize the cost of relocating almost every employee's workstation on average every nine months as a result of constantly changing business requirements. This was the most expensive option.

- *Balanced investment*: This proposed a design that was a little less robust and flexible but sufficiently resilient to ensure that technical availability targets would be met so that customer service and quality measures could be achieved. This would reduce the bank's capital outlay by 12 percent from the first option.

- *Rapid payback*: In this option we described a design that was simple but functional, with a basic level of resilience. The probability factor for technical unavailability fell slightly to 99.5 percent, and operational flexibility came with the need for the bank to assign more technical staff to manage the required level of churn and change. This option reduced the bank's capital outlay by 19 percent from the first option.

We spent a couple of hours presenting the three options and answering questions from the bank's negotiating team. All the questions were about the trade-off between initial investment and subsequent lifetime costs, how the three different designs would work in practice, and how risk could be managed both during the project and in subsequent live operations. There was no repeat of the earlier obsession with reducing the price. After a break to consult with other specialists, the bank came back with a proposal to go with the first option. With some minor trades, we were able to agree on penalties for over-run, ongoing technical training and support, and a guarantee that their choice of one of our client's project managers was to be assigned for the duration. We traded these for slightly bigger and earlier-stage payments, a lower retention fee with earlier release, and a great discount rate on fleet vehicle finance for our client!

Breaking a Negotiation Deadlock

At times, no matter how well you plan, the negotiation can seem to get into a deadlock where no progress appears to be possible. The main thing to remember is that both parties will lose if the deadlock is allowed to continue.

That's not to say that there are never commercial negotiations where the best course of action is simply to walk away. Sometimes it is better to have no resolution at all than to have one that is unsatisfactory to both parties. Clearly that is not what we want in hostage negotiation, but for now let's focus on commercial situations. Let's assume there is a mutual desire to reach an agreement that for the moment seems to be frustrated by some sort of deadlock. At these times there are a few techniques that can be tried to unlock the door to progress, as follows:

- *Recess:* Deadlock often happens when both parties reach a stage when they simply need a break. Take some time away from each other. You may also want to "phone a friend." You might benefit from some refreshments, or you may simply want to take your mind off the deal for a short time. In lengthy negotiations, you may want to catch some sleep, which often sparks a fresh perspective. It often happens that toward the end of the recess, other members of your support team will be able to suggest some ideas on how to get back on track.

- *Venue:* Often a change of venue will help. If you have been locked up in one place for a while, that may be contributing to the feeling of deadlock. Find another place: a different room, a different building, some other country if necessary. Sometimes a walk in the grounds is just the simple change that is needed.

- *Common ground:* You can occasionally get the negotiation going again by summarizing the common ground and restating the benefits that both parties can anticipate by resolving the conflict.

- *Mini-wins:* In most negotiations, there will be some elements of the deal that are not at all contentious to either party. Both sides can enjoy a small "win-win" if you go through these minor elements and reach easy agreement. That often starts to build a winning momentum that carries through into more substantial elements of the deal. However, if the other party seem overly keen to agree, it may be that what seems like a minor issue to you may be worth a lot to them, and you could use this as a lever to break the deadlock.

- *Ring-fence:* Find a way to temporarily isolate the most contentious elements of the deal and ring-fence these while you continue to make progress on other issues.

- *Small concessions:* If you have been saying no for a while, you may be perceived as the No Man, so try saying yes to a small concession. Remember that behavior breeds behavior.

- *Style:* A change of style is often appropriate. Remember that negotiation is cooperative rather than competitive. It may be that the perception of the other party has become locked into a view that you are being competitive. Try sitting up and showing them that you are interested. Reflect to them some key words that they use to encourage them to see that you are showing a more cooperative style.

- *Willingness:* Ask yourself how long it has been since you gave a willingness signal to the other party. A small movement, to indicate your potential willingness to concede in the right circumstances, can often help to free the logjam.

- *Ask why*: If you have already tried a few ideas where you have made the initial efforts, now may be the time to ask the other party why it is that they don't want to deal. At the least, this can help to get the conversation moving again. Use many open questions rather than closed questions to keep the dialogue open.

- *Off the record*: A good technique for clearing a deadlock is to ask if the session can go "off the record," requesting the suspension of the formal record taking by both teams. This may be particularly effective when combined with a break for example to "take a walk to stretch our legs." The danger here is that if some signs emerge of the deadlock being cleared, it may be difficult to recapture that willingness once you are back in the more formal setting when the notes are once more being written. It is important for the leader to be professional and fair and to be building a rapport that can be carried back to the table.

- *Specification*: It is often useful to consider changing the specification of the product or service in question. A small change can often be used as a lever to make more fundamental changes elsewhere and break the deadlock.

- *Timescales*: Often a certain key deadline or timescale can be at the heart of a deadlock. Sometimes a small shift of dates can help to unblock progress on other issues. Conversely, if the negotiation has already dragged on too long, setting even an arbitrary deadline can focus attention on clearing a logjam.

- *Contract*: When there is already a contract, or a draft contract, a suggested change to certain clauses can help to free the deadlock.

- *Reframe the language*: Often there is a deadlock on a certain issue because the language used to describe the respective positions alienates the parties involved. Try reframing the language to avoid emotional terms. For example, a trade union may refuse even to discuss an employer's proposal to "Cut pension benefits" but find it more acceptable to discuss how to "Protect jobs by agreeing on necessary economies."

- *Risk*: In many negotiations there are finely balanced perceptions of relative risk between the parties. If you can suggest a slight change in the division of risk taking, you will often find that the other party will respond well to the movement.

- *Finance*: Even though many negotiations place too much emphasis on the financial elements, it is often the case that a change in the financial terms can help to free up some concessions on other key elements of the deal.

- *Subgroup*: If the deadlock is over just a minority of the issues and the negotiating teams are large, try forming a subgroup of just one or two from each team to break away from the main negotiation session with the aim of resolving the minority problems while the main negotiation continues.

- *Third party*: Sometimes the introduction of a third party can help to overcome a deadlock. That is not to say that the negotiation turns into arbitration. You need to define the role of the third party clearly so this does not happen. A new face can often make a big difference in changing the dynamics and atmosphere of the negotiation.

- *Referee*: In some negotiations that are deadlocked on just one last issue, it can help to bring in an independent referee on this one sticking point. It is often possible for conflicted parties to compromise to a referee rather than directly to the other party.

- *New team*: In an extreme deadlock, it may become necessary to change one or more of the members of the team or even the leader.

Cross-Cultural Issues in Negotiation

Over the past three decades we have witnessed a gradual increase in what could be called cross-cultural negotiation. As our clients increasingly acquire resources and services from the global market and sell to other businesses across the world, there is a need for a negotiation model that can bridge those diverse cultures. Everything so far in this book has been as culturally neutral as possible, and our negotiation techniques are applicable across a wide range of locations. We will now deal with some specific considerations that you should build into your planning when negotiating with people from cultures you may not have dealt with before. In doing this, we run the risk of making generalizations and discussing stereotypes that may be unfair and inaccurate. However, be assured that we intend no insult to any culture or tradition whatsoever.

Behavior and Cultural Differences

The first stage is to try to assess the extent to which culture may influence the other party's behavior. You will want to minimize the risk of cultural misunderstanding. If possible, find out whether they are experienced in dealing with people from your background and culture because this may give them an advantage over you. If you have little relevant cross-cultural experience, consider engaging an advisor from the other party's culture to help you in your planning phase and to provide you with support during the negotiation.

You may also need to engage a local lawyer to help with any cross-border contracts that will need to specify which country's law will apply, to clarify local custom and practice, or to explain standard terms that are routinely included in contracts. You should not agree to any standard terms until after due research and consideration as part of the negotiation.

You may be able to control many aspects of the negotiation in advance. For example, you can select the most appropriate people to be members of your team. Sometimes you may have control over the venue and start time, which may be important to help you avoid beginning the negotiation with jet lag from traveling across several time zones. Be aware that if the other party is suffering from jet lag, they may be less receptive even to your "win-win" approach. Resist any temptation to accept entertainment by the other party prior to the negotiation in case this exacerbates your jet lag or travel weariness. It may be best to plan to arrive at your hotel a couple of days in advance, without telling your hosts, to give yourself time to adjust to the local time and climate. If this is not possible, consider adjusting your body clock in incremental phases over a couple of days before you leave by moving a few hours closer to your target time zone simply by waking, eating, and going to sleep a little later or earlier as appropriate.

If you can't do this, then we have found a few simple rules can help you to minimize the effects of jet lag. First, at the earliest opportunity, set your watch, telephone, and other electronic devices to your target local time and begin to eat and sleep in that zone. Avoid eating the last meal scheduled for your old time zone and decline the main meals on the plane; don't drink alcohol or caffeinated beverages, but have plenty of still water. As soon as you arrive in the target zone, break your fast with whatever is the current local meal—breakfast, lunch, dinner or supper—to begin to adjust to the rhythm. If your negotiation has sent you east, try to get to sleep early and then get up early and walk in the early morning sun if there is any. If your negotiation has sent you west, try to get an hour's walk in the light before you go to bed.

You may also be able to control the issues on the negotiation agenda and even the language in which it will be conducted. For example, our experience has been that if you are buying from a German-speaking culture, the other party will almost always speak your language. However, if you are selling into a German-speaking culture, you may find it is an advantage to negotiate in that language. If none of your team has the necessary skills, that immediately raises the question of how best to arrange interpreters. In most cases, you would be advised to hire your own interpreter rather than try to rely on the other party's facilities. You will need to check credentials and references from an independent source. It may be best to avoid using local agents who may have a vested interest in the outcome of the negotiation because they may even inadvertently bias their interpretation one way or the other. Be aware of the difference between interpreters who you will need for the live action and translators who you will need for any written material. Interpreters may not fully grasp the subtleties of meaning in the terminology you use in your business, so you will need to plan and pay for the time necessary to get them up to speed.

During the sessions, you will need to talk more carefully and a little slower than usual. Avoid long rambling sentences and pause more often to give the interpreter a chance to translate accurately what you have said. When you are listening, don't just listen to the interpreter. It is important to show the speaker that you are actively listening to them and not just to the interpreter. Sit up and look toward the speaker to show you are interested. Try to hear the tone of voice used by the other party, maintain eye contact with them, and watch out for body language signals. Don't overreact to these cues because you won't know enough about the individuals to be sure what sort of body language is "normal" for them, and you may not be familiar with their cultural content. Many Asian and African cultures traditionally offer respect by looking down and avoiding lengthy, direct eye contact. In contrast, many people from Europe, North America, and the Middle East may unconsciously interpret this as inattentiveness, disrespect, or even deception. The converse of this is that people from some Asian and African cultures may unconsciously feel that people from Europe, North America, and the Middle East often glare at them disrespectfully.

If you are not happy with what you hear from the interpreter or the feedback from the other party, reword your message and try again. If you are worried about missing part of what the other party said, don't hesitate to double-check. Expect both parties to have to spend time clarifying what they meant and what they didn't mean. Don't assume that because you have been communicating through an interpreter, nobody from the other party can understand your language. Assume that everything you say within your own team can be overheard and understood, especially things you had hoped were confidential.

Even when both parties apparently speak the same language, we have often found important cultural differences. For example, negotiators from the United States and the United Kingdom can easily misunderstand each other. An example of this during a negotiation was when we heard the American leader ask if we would agree to "table" a particular issue. In the United Kingdom, that would mean that we were being invited to place the issue on the main negotiating table and discuss it right away, even if it was an item that was not previously included on the formal agenda. However, in most of the United States, to "table" an issue means to take it off the current agenda and place it on a side table to be discussed at some later time. That sort of problem can arise at any time, and you need to be aware of this and to be flexible in your responses.

There is another type of language problem: body language. Consider also that there are often differences between the way men and women can act in a single culture let alone across traditions. For example, in negotiations, women tend to nod their head to signal that they are actively listening. This is not meant to indicate their agreement with what is being said. Men tend to be less concerned about letting you know they are listening and may sit passively, nodding their head occasionally only when they want to signal that they agree. Research has indicated that some cultures in parts of India, Greece, Bulgaria, and Turkey traditionally associated a slightly different meaning to head nods and wobbles than does the rest of the world, but our experience is that business people from these cultures are well aware of this and are careful to be clear. However, the key message is to not assume that someone agrees or disagrees with what you're saying; be sure to ask explicitly.

Research indicates that negotiators from the United States often communicate their objectives and desires much more directly than do British or Japanese negotiators and sometimes don't understand why the British and Japanese appear reticent. You may find that Japanese negotiators have a formal sense of respect and humility that can come across as a tendency to be self-critical or even disparaging of their own company and products. This is not meant to be literal but simply a way of showing that they are not arrogant. The Japanese teams are usually much better at reading between the lines and are generally quick to grasp key information and suggest ways of creating value for both parties. This is not as common in negotiators from Hong Kong who are sometimes reluctant to share enough information to make this happen. Russian negotiators may often come across as competitive and perhaps adversarial, employing their power base more rigorously than, say, a British team. However, they will take the time to try to build relationships. Negotiators from the United States can appear to be overly competitive and may take some time to come around to a more cooperative approach to value creation, but this can depend on the region in which you are working. For example, many negotiators from parts of the Northeast and the West Coast may be more competitive and appear aggressive, whereas we have found that negotiators from the Midwest and the South often appear to have a stronger focus on relationships. They are more likely to use fudging phrases that we're more used to hearing from the British. Rather than saying simply no, we often hear people saying "Oh, I'm not sure if I can agree with that point right now." However, our experience of negotiators from the United States is of a great diversity of styles, and we see more differences between companies than between one state and another. Generally, the pace of negotiation is fast, and the focus is on current deals and profits rather than on building personal relationships. Our clients in the United States appear to enter into litigation more often than clients do elsewhere in the world, so our recommendation would be to make sure that, in any sizable negotiations, you include advice from a relevant expert lawyer.

Some cultures have a history of making extreme offers in the hope of lowering the expectations of the other party. In parts of China, expect buyers to offer you a very low price, and expect sellers to demand a very high price. This is often just an opening gambit that may influence an inexperienced negotiator into a concession. Some communities in China have a tradition of reinforcing discipline and education through "shaming," which other cultures may perceive as too negative a technique of reinforcement. This approach may encourage some negotiators from China to try to leverage your mistakes by taking a superior stance in the expectation that by losing face you will be compelled into concessions. You will probably find that the pace of negotiation in China is much slower than in the United States, and there will often be a strong focus on building relationships and the cultivation of trust. Many other cultures do not share this emphasis on relationships and may misunderstand it as wasting time because they are keen to press on with the subject. In an attempt to respect the other party by not wasting their time, they may lose that respect by failing to engage at a human level.

Another contrast we see between negotiators from China and the United States is the ease with which we are able to link together a couple of our "jellyfish" elements. We often find it useful in negotiations to trade one element off against another in the total package. However, in the United States and to a lesser extent in the United Kingdom, we generally find negotiators wanting to treat each element of the deal as if it were in its own isolated little box, whereas in China and in the Middle East it appears to be accepted and welcomed for the negotiation to range flexibly from one element to another and back again, exploring potential linkages and offsets.

Some cultures are highly collective, while others are more highly individualistic. For example, negotiators from Taiwan may often focus on creating and maintaining personal relationships. This can manifest itself within the members of the team from Taiwan and also between the two negotiating parties. A subordinate will generally not interrupt the leader in a negotiation, even if the leader has clearly gotten something wrong. The team from Taiwan may present a united front to the extent that they suppress their individual ideas until a break in the proceedings provides the opportunity for them to discuss issues in private. That emphasizes the importance of scheduling frequent pauses and for calling for unscheduled breaks when you believe these are needed either for your team or for the other party.

In general, the more collectivist, high-context cultures lay greater emphasis on mutual relations, and in many Asian and African cultures there is a tradition of welcoming guests with food and gifts and providing entertainment. The exchange of personal favors is more prevalent than in typical western cultures. This tradition can often manifest itself in negotiations and may be misinterpreted by people from different traditions. In many African and Latin

American societies, showing emotion is a normal aspect and means of communication, but this can also be misinterpreted by people from more individualistic cultures, which attach more importance to the apparent suppression of emotion under a veneer of logic and rationality. Collectivist cultures are more likely to take into account the authority and power position of negotiators and emotional dimensions of the deal. We have also noticed while in West Africa and the Caribbean that keeping to agreed-upon time schedules can be difficult. People seem to assume that everything will take twice as long as planned and that everyone will understand if urgent family matters cause delays to the start of a session.

We've mentioned head nodding, but other body language is also important. During our first negotiation in the Middle East many years ago, we felt that the formal sessions around the table were going quite well, but the atmosphere before we sat down was a little tense, and every time we had a break or refreshments, the tension built up again. When we had the chance to ask our local advisor about this, we were told to pick a point on the floor and lock our feet onto the spot no matter what happened. As people from the other party approached us to chat informally, we found they came into very close physical proximity. At home we would have felt this was too close an invasion of our personal space. Previously we had been unconsciously backing off a little until we were more comfortable. However, the other party would then feel uncomfortable with that bigger gap and so would shuffle closer until they felt they were leaving the appropriate smaller gap, at which point we would slip a little further away. In the Middle East, people of the same gender tend to stand much closer to each other than do people from Europe and North America, while people of the opposite gender tend to stand much further apart. Once we understood these differences, we were able to compensate, and the negotiation was successful. A similar example is that Japanese men tend to stand well over an arm's length apart when having a discussion, while people from Europe and North America usually stand about an arm's length apart.

The extent to which people from different cultures expect to touch and be touched varies considerably. People from Asia and the Middle East and from Britain generally shake hands at the start and end of a session and have almost no physical contact in between. In contrast, people from North America tend to add other contacts such as laying a hand on a shoulder or arm several times during a discussion, and people from France and Italy will do this more often. If you will be eating meals with the other party, be aware that there may be some differences in traditions that may conspire to make you uncomfortable, so do your research and be prepared. Take your cues from the people around you. For example, you may find that Japanese negotiators are very happy to eat and talk enthusiastically at the same time, whereas somebody from the

United Kingdom will not want to "talk with their mouth full." Many cultures avoid using the left hand for eating, so watch what other people are doing and follow their lead.

Having said all that, our experience has been that despite the many interesting and rich differences between cultures and traditions, the act of coming together in a commercial negotiation usually means that both parties are already on more or less the same wavelength. They may disagree on the issues but are usually ready to be understanding and flexible and to make allowances for mistakes. Most people we have dealt with are more likely than not to find humor in the occasional cultural collision.

The Rule of Law Index

If you are debating the opportunities for negotiating commercial deals in countries that are new to you, it may be helpful for you to look at the *Rule of Law Index* published by the World Justice Project. This provides a free guide to the extent to which about 100 countries across the world adhere to the rule of law in practice. The index can help you decide whether your hard-won commercial agreements will be supported by the local laws and can be enforced in practice when necessary through a process that is not prohibitively expensive or time-consuming. The annual reports issued by the World Justice Project consider a wide range of relevant factors but can be simplified and summarized in a few key concepts, for example: that laws are enacted fairly and are clear, publicized, stable, and just; that they are applied fairly to protect the security of people, property, and commercial interests; that government officials and agents of commercial organizations are accountable under the law; and that justice is delivered by competent, ethical, and independent representatives of society.

A little research should help you to be prepared to negotiate well in countries that are new to you and to be aware of how easily contracts can be enforced, the extent of bribery and corruption, organized crime, black markets, the quality of police, and the likelihood of crime and violence.

Hostage Negotiation Perspective

In this chapter, the meaning of the term *hostage negotiation* can be broadened to embrace crisis negotiation of several types, including threatened suicide or self-harm. A separate type of scenario may be kidnap for money, where the analogy to commercial negotiation may perhaps be strongest. There are mutual lessons to be learned from the different perspectives of commercial and hostage negotiation. Much of this book has been informed by several types of negotiations and in turn is applicable to all of these. There are so many widely different scenarios within the various realms of negotiation that the otherwise separate disciplines have some overlaps between them in some areas. Don't just think of hostage negotiation as being about one person holding a gun to another in a bank. Consider the situation in the middle of tribal negotiations over access to safe artesian water when suddenly armed protagonists seize the only well for miles around while a woman and child are there. In that way, what begins as a commercial negotiation has the potential to deteriorate into a hostage negotiation. Consider also what happens when a retail food company is taken hostage by people contaminating products in its store. Think of the reputation of a show business celebrity being taken hostage by media phone hacking. Finally, think about employees of an oil exploration company taken hostage by modern-day pirates seeking a ransom. These are just some examples of different forms of hostage situations.

Different Types of Negotiation

There are at least three big areas of differences between hostage negotiation and commercial negotiation: the start, the middle, and the end. At the start, in hostage negotiation there are unacceptable consequences of us failing to at least try to agree a resolution, whereas in commercial negotiation we usually have the option of avoiding the situation. In the middle, hostage negotiation is often saturated with raw emotion to a far greater extent than in commercial situations. Finally, at the end of commercial negotiations people generally shake hands, sign the contract, deliver the goods, and get paid. At the end of hostage negotiations, people often get thrown to the ground, handcuffed, and hauled off to a state institution. However, despite these differences, there are many similarities between commercial and hostage negotiations. One similarity is that in all negotiations the aim is for everyone to come out at the end with their pride and dignity intact. Even at the end of most hostage situations, the resolution is often discussed and agreed on with the hostage takers so they feel they have contributed to the plan and can accept that they will have to be handcuffed because that is the standard procedure for the law enforcement agencies.

Let's consider differences between hostage and commercial negotiation from the start point of purpose and motives. The purpose in a commercial context is the voluntary and systematic exploration of both parties' interests with the objective of agreeing on a mutually acceptable compromise that resolves their conflict and may even create additional profits above and beyond those that either of the parties could generate in isolation. It's not very productive to think about motivation in hostage situations in terms of the good guys versus the bad guys because there are so many possible scenarios, ranging from domestic disputes and barricaded individuals to threatened suicide or self-harm to kidnappings and extortions to prison riots and sieges. We need to make a distinction between situations where victims are merely "instrumental" in the sense that, to the hostage takers, they represent a means to an end, rather than situations where hostage takers believe they have a personal relationship with their victim. There may be emotional, political, or religious motivations alongside financial ones. A politically motivated hostage taker may want publicity for their cause, may want to undermine the confidence of society, or may want to free other members of the organization held in prison. However, we can simplify the picture by considering the public's stereotypical example of one person holding a gun on others in a bank. The superficial motive may seem to be greed, but there is often an underlying motive; and as the situation develops, the motives become confused with fear and the desire to escape. A hostage taker may often be suffering from a temporary suspension of their problem-solving ability. In many hostage negotiations, the "conflict" may be an internal mental state, and the "resolution" may be the restoration of rational coping functions.

The professional negotiator sent to deal with the hostage taker is in one sense a representative of society, and as a courtesy we won't speculate on their personal motivation, but we will consider what they are hoping to achieve. Their purpose may be to free the hostages and have the hostage taker submit to the society's justice system. The aim is always to get everyone out alive. If the negotiation breaks down and a rescue attempt has to be made, then law enforcement officers will have to put their own lives at risk, alongside the hostages and the hostage takers. In these circumstances there is always a chance that someone will get killed or seriously wounded. On the other hand, if the negotiation can be concluded successfully, then everyone can come out alive and uninjured.

When lives are directly at stake, emotions are bound to run high. In addition, the motivation driving many hostage takers appears to be emotional anxieties and relationship problems. Their overt demands may be for a helicopter and a suitcase full of money, but they may often be just seeking attention and respect. The negotiators have learned to listen attentively to the hostage taker and work from the overt demands to try to build rapport so they can begin to understand the underlying motivation and get to the root of the problem. There is little point in appealing for a rational discussion based on facts rather than perceptions. When a person can no longer cope and enters a crisis state, their normal rational state seems to subsume under pure emotion. Thinking seems to be replaced by action. However, it is often possible to help the person to gradually reconnect with their rational coping functions and to reactivate their normal problem-solving abilities. Hostage negotiation can be described by the following main activities: establish communication, develop rapport, buy time, gather information, defuse the emotion, build influence, and finally reach resolution.

The first step, once the situation has been contained, is to open up a dialogue. The hostage negotiator shows the hostage takers that they care about them simply by being there and listening to them. Empathy is expressed, and rapport is attempted by reflecting back to the hostage takers their own comments. When the negotiators hear "Nobody listens; nobody cares; there's nothing else I can do," they may show concern by explaining how they sometimes feel isolated too. They may use a variety of expressions to keep the dialogue open and to begin to build rapport, such as the following: "If I were in your situation, I would be upset" or "I have the impression that you feel very isolated" or "It sounds to me that you are understandably anxious." The negotiators can also say that although they've never been in such a situation, they can "begin to imagine how depressed and lonely you must be feeling." In this way, a bond is slowly established, and from this a relationship is gradually built. Open questions will be asked to ensure the hostage taker keeps on talking and eventually volunteers useful information.

Similarities and Lessons to Learn

Much of this is similar to the commercial negotiation mantras discussed earlier, as shown in Figure 12-1.

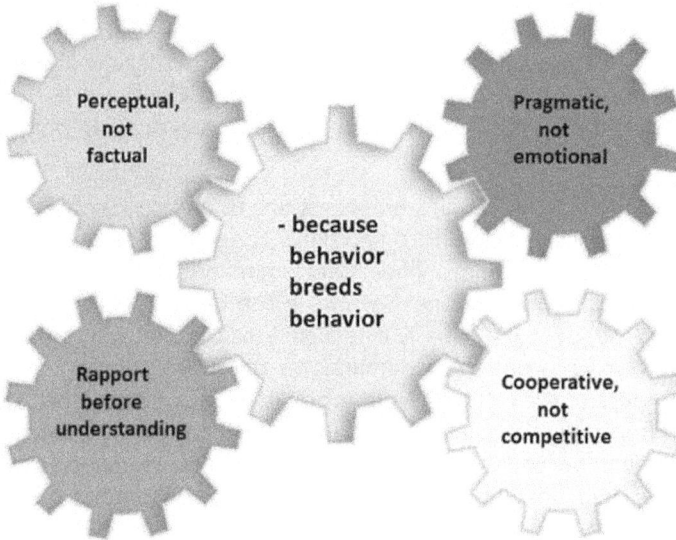

Figure 12-1. RDB negotiation mantras

The negotiator talks to buy time in which to help the hostage takers to gradually discuss the situation until they can think more clearly and become more receptive. They may explore what possibly triggered the crisis, although in some situations this may be judged to be too sensitive. In time, as the emotional state subsides, the hostage negotiator will look for opportunities to help the hostage takers to reconnect with their rational coping functions.

As time goes by, the negotiator will be expecting mini-demands such as for food and will be ready to use these mini-negotiations in order to find ways to discuss, propose, trade, and agree. The idea is to create small successes where both parties have worked together so that trust can gradually be built and later used as a lever to influence the hostage taker on more substantial issues. These mini-negotiations are the direct analogy of the commercial negotiation model we have already covered, as shown in Figure 12-2.

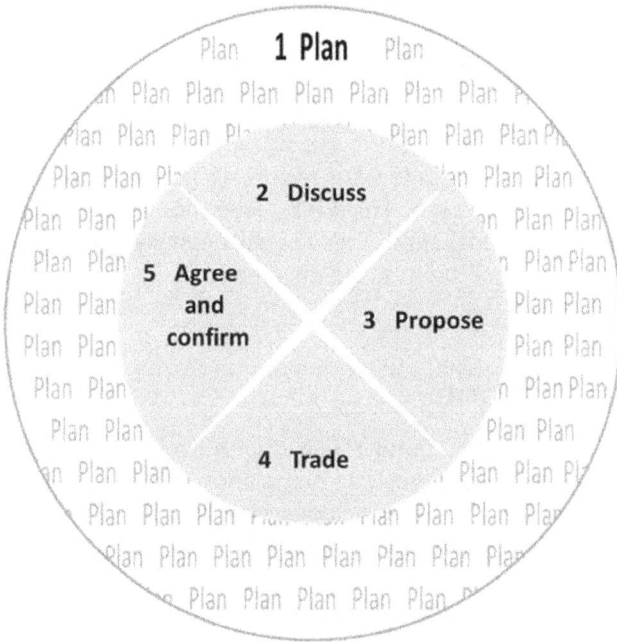

Figure 12-2. The five phases of negotiation

Many of the ten golden rules also apply: don't negotiate with yourself, don't accept the first offer, don't make the first offer if you can help it, listen more and talk less, don't give free gifts, and so on. In the propose and trade phases, each concession must be paid for by an equally valued concession. For example, we'll agree to send in some meals if you agree to free one of the hostages. These mini-negotiations and small successes allow the hostage negotiator to gradually build up the trust of the hostage takers and establish a momentum of positive experiences. This will be important later as if it were accumulated currency that can be spent in a valid attempt to influence the hostage takers on substantial issues such as how the hostage situation is to be ended.

One other difference between commercial and hostage negotiation is that in the latter, the victims may interact with both parties and become an active third party in the complex situation. The victims may directly influence the resolution in a way that happens less often with other types of third parties in the commercial world.

The final stage of the hostage negotiation is to work out an acceptable reso- lution and put it into action. This can be called a *coming-out plan*. In hostage negotiation, the superficial conflict and resolution may be about the hostages and the money, but the underlying "conflict" is often an internal mental state, and the "resolution" may be the restoration of rational coping functions. A good result is when the hostage taker eventually discusses, internalizes, agrees, and actions a coming-out plan. Thankfully, even though there are a large num- ber of hostage situations, almost all are successfully resolved without loss of life. It's just the small percentage that ends badly that catch the public's attention.

Kidnap for Money

The scenario we have not spent much time examining is kidnap for money, where the analogy to commercial negotiation may perhaps be strongest. However, on closer analysis, the analogy may not be so direct. In particular, there may be no negotiation involved at all. It could be classified as a selling and buying deal. The kidnappers may simply want to sell back the life of the person they have kidnapped, and the family or business associates may want to buy back the victim at any price. The only issue is whether the kidnappers actually have accurate information about how much money could be raised. Let's assume that the situation is not so straightforward and that a negotiation is necessary.

There may be several people who could be negotiating on behalf of the kid- nap victim and their family or business. The type of negotiation depends very much on who takes on the role of principal negotiator. Often this is a profes- sional who has experience of previous kidnap for money scenarios and who has been contracted through the victim's insurance company. However, there is still a great deal of emotion in the situation from family members and busi- ness associates who can't be excluded from the scenario. They are the ones who own the conflict along with the hostage takers; these people from both parties have heightened emotional states, and they are stakeholders in the resolution. The family and friends will ultimately pay the money, or, if things go badly wrong, they will potentially pay the greater price in loss of life.

Another difference between a normal commercial negotiation and one involv- ing kidnap for money is that the initiative and momentum is with the kidnap- pers. They have violently forced the situation on everyone else. There is little choice for the family but to enter into this negotiation. The pace of the nego- tiation is also set by the kidnappers, as is the location, the language, and almost every other dimension. This is in strong contrast with normal commercial deals, where there is usually a lot more choice for both parties. However, there are some parallels. There is a conflict, and it may require systematic exploration of both parties' interests with the objective of agreeing a mutually acceptable compromise that resolves the conflict. There may emerge several negotiable elements. The kidnappers may want a rapid resolution because the longer this drags on, the more chance there is that something will go wrong. They may have invested what is to them a great deal of money in the kidnap so far, and every day costs them more. On the other side, the family or business associates may have nowhere near the sum of money that is demanded and no way to raise such a sum. Even if they could possibly raise the cash, the professional negotiator may caution that they should beware of settling right away. Some of the ten golden rules for successful negotiation may be relevant. Rule 3 says never accept the first offer. If kidnappers demand $100,000 and the family instantly agrees, what's to stop the demand from being doubled?

Rule 4 says never make the first offer if you can avoid it. If the family knows they can raise only a maximum of $1 million and offer this, the danger is that the kidnappers see this as an opening gambit and demand ten times that sum, hoping to settle somewhere in the middle, which is completely unattainable to the family. Other relevant rules are: listen more and talk less, never give a free gift, avoid a quick deal, and never disclose your bottom line (they may come back for the rest in a second kidnapping).

Conclusions on the Hostage Perspective

In the past decade, there have been some interesting observations made of various types of hostage situations, along with interviews with negotiators such as police officers. Analysis of these experiences has indicated a wide range of different behaviors that may influence the other party in a negotiation. You may come across some of these behaviors in commercial negotiations, to a greater or lesser extent. In our experience, the more positive behaviors toward the top of the list are the most successful, but you should also be aware of the other more negative behaviors that you may be exposed to. Appendix B provides a table showing a list of ten categories of influence behavior (Dutch Journal of Psychology, 2002), which we have paraphrased and summarized as follows:

- Being respectful, kind, friendly, and helpful
- Identifying things the parties have in common
- Showing expertise, proving you are reliable and trustworthy
- Referring to the social rules we accept in order to live peacefully
- Using give-and-take behavior

- Using persuasive arguments and logic

- Understanding or manipulating the emotions of the other party

- Delaying or making something available in a limited way

- Staying resistant to pressure or exerting it in a neutral manner

- Threatening with punishment or accusing the other party

To draw some conclusions from this chapter, we have seen there are many surprising similarities and some productive differences between commercial negotiation and hostage negotiation. There are some interesting differences of perspective and emphasis that can provide mutual lessons to be learned. You can see that much of this book has been informed by both types of negotiations and in turn is applicable to both. It's now time to extend this comparison to embrace the perspective of diplomatic negotiation in the following chapter.

Diplomatic Negotiation Perspective

The diplomatic services of some countries have a working definition of diplomacy that excludes the word *negotiation* because they don't like the connotations of that term. They feel that, at worst, the role of a negotiator is to bamboozle the enemy at their front door while your military forces kick down their back door! They see the purpose of practical diplomacy as being to clean up the mess that nations all too often get themselves into by trying to deceive one another and impose a "win-lose" result in so-called negotiations. This resonates with the ethos we have discussed throughout this book, where the objective of principled negotiation is a "win-win" that aims to ensure that all parties to the negotiation realize they have achieved the best possible results. This approach seeks to create additional value above and beyond the value that either of the parties involved in the negotiation could find in isolation. In comparing the functions of diplomatic and commercial negotiation, it is interesting to note that individual businesses could not effectively conduct commercial negotiations without the global infrastructure that is constantly updated and maintained by diplomatic negotiations. At one end of the scale, that infrastructure seeks to avoid war, while at the other end of the scale it paves the way for international law, contracts, finance, transport, and profit. But there is also a negative dimension. Countries can decide to ban trade of certain types such as military and strategic technology. They can choose to impose sanctions on other states, perhaps restricting credit, transport, and other infrastructure facilities. They can set prohibitive trade tariffs and quotas on certain classes of goods. So, in many ways, commercial negotiations can be successful only under the facilitating umbrella of diplomatic negotiation.

Perhaps more surprisingly, there is also a positive link in the opposite direction because statistics show that pairs of nations that trade more extensively with each other are also highly motivated to avoid war with their commercial partners. It may be that conducting many commercial negotiations helps people from one nation to conceptualize the points of view of people from the other nation. It seems that becoming committed to mutual business obligations makes it less likely that nations will dehumanize each other, and therefore less likely to wage war, and more likely to realize the advantages of sharing a "peace dividend."

There are mutual lessons to be learned from the different perspectives of commercial and diplomatic negotiation. Of course, we won't find the world's leading diplomats blogging their negotiation techniques on the Internet! We don't expect to see their social network pages telling us how they really fooled country X in a massive bluff this week or that they were embarrassed by how well their counterparty from rogue state Y managed to identify their point of resistance. A great deal of effort goes into keeping secret the training and operational tactics that have been developed by countries over many centuries and the skills that have been developed by individual negotiators over many years. The timescales involved can be very long, with international laws taking decades to negotiate and wars taking many years to transition from the battlefield into a disarmament agreement lodged in the United Nations Treaty Library.

Diplomatic negotiations between countries or agencies are sometimes as serious as ensuring the survival of people and states. More often, it's about resolving divergent values and conflicts of interests that frequently erupt. States have a wide range of possible interests, such as access to energy, raw materials, water, food, credit, and trade. In commercial negotiations, the focus is often on price because money is easy to count, whereas the other negotiable elements may be more difficult to quantify objectively. Therefore, a simple common yardstick is monetary value. Nonfinancial criteria are often reduced to potential future cash flows, discounted to present-day values. In diplomatic negotiations, there may appear to be less overt focus on money and more on longer-term issues such as survival, prestige, and cultural identity. Yet the immediate issues are often about access to critical resources that, in the end, force the focal point back onto the common yardstick of money. In any conflict, even when it has huge humanitarian dimensions, politicians and the public will always want to know whether their country "has a dog in this fight," in other words, whether their national interests could be frustrated or promoted by the potential outcomes.

As with individual people, nations may also be quite capable of self-deception and may appear to be blind to the counterparty's valid perceptions and positions. In particular, there may be significant differences in the way that a harm received from the counterparty is described compared to a harm done to the counterparty. A harm received is often described in emotional language and almost reverent terms, and the memories of the events are often passed down to future generations in terms of sadness and awe that can still provoke anger. In contrast, a harm done to the counterparty may be described in a way that seeks to understate the impact of the events and to explain away the actions as being necessary to avoid a greater harm or as a justifiable reaction to an aggression by the counterparty. We often see something similar to this in a commercial context when two organizations have been in a series of separate negotiations over an extended period. If one party feels they have suffered an unacceptable "lose-win" in one negotiation, it seems almost as if the organization develops its own memory that retains an imprint of a score that needs to be settled in the next negotiation. This leads to a downward spiral of reducing value, which often can be reversed only by major changes in both organizations. In the same way that nations often make progress toward reconciliation only after their respective heads of state have left office, organizations can sometimes regain an upward spiral of mutual benefits only once the lead negotiators have been replaced or the chief executives have moved on!

There is sometimes a slightly different vocabulary used to describe diplomatic negotiation compared to commercial negotiation. We see words such as *threat, aggression, problem, situation,* and *dispute.* There are terms such as *counterparty, point of resistance, empathy, convince, bargaining,* and so on. However, the underlying concepts and principles are similar. Perhaps we should not be surprised that there are strong parallels, given that for centuries there was little distinction between diplomatic and commercial negotiations—often with the same people conducting the proceedings.

The traditions of diplomatic negotiators include careful research and planning. They know how information can flow through their own organizations and will find out how information and influence flow within the counterparty's various organizations. They will also be aware that third-party states, international agencies, and the press can often be used as deniable "back channels" for leaking positions that if necessary can be subsequently dismissed as false. Sometimes diplomatic negotiations suffer from too much direct political attention from the top, while progress can often be made along a depoliticized technical channel. Similarly, the commercial negotiator needs to be aware of the other party's official, structured flows and should research the other informal relationships that may be even more important than those that are documented on the organizational charts.

Diplomatic negotiation is often about the resolution of differences and disputes by peaceful means to reduce the possibility of either party resorting to even the limited use of force that has the potential to escalate into war. The aim is for convergent, agreed-upon action to resolve divergent values and conflicts of interests, even though this may be achieved only by both sides making compromises. The motivation of either side to reach a settlement is sometimes to bolster their political power at home. Often it is to encourage their citizens' good opinion of their government's flexibility and competence. They may want to maintain their state's influence in regional organizations or avoid having its credibility and power reduced on the international stage. Finally, they may want to avoid upsetting their allies or provoking neutral states and agencies. All these considerations provide motivation for a settlement. However, in the end, diplomatic negotiators compromise because they believe there is more value to them in the concessions they receive than in the ones they give in exchange. In that sense, there is no difference between the "bargaining" in diplomatic negotiations and the "trading" in commercial negotiations; they both follow the model discussed in this material, and all of the ten golden rules for successful negotiation are relevant. For example, the first rule is not to negotiate unless you need to do so. In commerce, you should prefer to buy or sell well whenever possible rather than compromise. In diplomacy, you should prefer to reach a settlement whenever possible without compromise.

The similarity continues when we consider the competencies and behaviors of diplomatic negotiators. To be fully effective, they need to have a clear vision of their mission and its goals and a well-developed ability to communicate their objectives. They are strong defenders of their own state or agency and competent protectors of its security and interests. They need to know their own country's bottom line and at what point diplomacy may give way to force. Both sides study their counterparties and research their motivations, needs, and negotiating styles. They plan how best to question and elicit the counterparty's expectations and their views of the situation. They develop a rapport to help them identify attitudes, feelings about important issues, and pressures being exerted by the counterparty's superiors. All this will help them to determine the probable point of resistance—the minimum that the counterparty might accept as a resolution. The relevant lesson to be carried from diplomatic to commercial negotiation is to dedicate an appropriate amount of time and effort in the planning stage, commensurate with the potential risks and rewards.

Perhaps there are a couple of areas of marked difference between commercial and diplomatic negotiations; there may be an element of bluff in some situations, requiring diplomatic negotiators to develop a strong personal relationship with the counterparty and convince them that they are "super-trustworthy" right up to the point when the bluff may be exposed. A second tactic is initially to refuse to negotiate and then provoke an incident so that crisis negotiation becomes necessary at a point when the counterparty may be so anxious to reach an agreement that they offer compromises they would not have considered in normal circumstances. These are not tactics we feel are productive in commercial negotiations, but there are times when the other party may try these tricks and so you should be wary of them.

Diplomatic negotiators will avoid being sympathetic because this brings the danger of too close an emotional bond, but they will develop empathy so they can imagine what the situation feels like from the counterparty's perspective. They will explore the ways in which the two potentially conflicting agendas can be made to appear more compatible. They will listen carefully and look for opportunities to develop a relationship where they can take the counterparty into their confidence on certain issues. The intention is to encourage the counterparty to also open up and bring our negotiators into their confidence. They will search for ways to assist the counterparty to achieve their objectives as long as this helps our negotiators to achieve our goals. They will sustain an untiring effort to communicate and seek understanding, trying to convince the counterparty of the legitimacy and logic of our stance and explaining why it is that our values and interests are so important to us. All this demands unbounded patience and resilience, not least because the counterparty will often try to manipulate the world media to denigrate the other state and launch personal attacks on individual negotiators. On occasions, we have seen all of these factors and tactics, both good and bad, also being used in commercial negotiations.

Diplomatic negotiators will use their bargaining skills to make conditional offers and seek concessions, using incentives and disincentives, and will forge a link between the issues currently on the negotiating table and other issues that might also be brought into the bargaining position. Sometimes, a state may be unable to agree to concessions it knows that it can and should make because it would lose too much face, not just with its population but also with other countries and agencies. In these circumstances, diplomatic negotiators may agree to mask the details of any concessions through confidentiality clauses.

This may also be used in some commercial negotiations to avoid competitors and prospects from learning about potential concessions or to protect a company's public image. For example, we have seen this done in software license agreements where the customer has inadvertently or willfully exceeded the number of "seats" allowed under the license. The supplier generally wants to retain the revenue stream from the customer and may be reluctant to accuse them of theft. But they may subtly apply the threat of public exposure in order to pressure the customer into accepting a negotiated multiple-year deal at the list price for a single year, with no discounts. In effect, the previous year's transgression may be paid for by rolling forward the obligation disguised as a new deal. When a company's reputation is threatened by bad publicity, its staff engaged in a negotiation may place so much emphasis on managing their business image that they forget they are still in a negotiation.

Throughout a diplomatic negotiation, one or both parties can often maintain a threat as a deterrent or as an incentive to compromise. Sometimes the threat is very real, and at other times it may be a bluff, but the diplomatic negotiators need to be able to employ brinkmanship without losing control and tottering over the edge. This is not something we feel is useful in commercial negotiations, but there are times when the other party may try to emphasize the power they have in the negotiation by reminding you how difficult it would be for you to find another suitable supplier quickly or another key customer in time to hit your annual targets.

Finally, there is a striking difference between diplomatic and commercial negotiations regarding the percentage of time actually spent in the main sessions with the parties face to face. Diplomatic negotiators often spend only a small percentage of the total time sitting across the table from each other. Most of the time is spent in recess so that each team can, in private, discuss progress and tactics and plan what their next few moves are going to be. Often we find that in commercial negotiations this percentage is reversed, with people spending most of their time around the table. The lesson to be learned is to have frequent breaks and use this time to consult discreetly with your immediate team and if necessary with other supporters onsite or at the other end of the telephone. Review and update your plans and make sure the whole team knows what needs to be done in the next session.

In conclusion, there are many similarities and some interesting differences of perspective and emphasis that can provide mutual lessons to be learned in commercial, diplomatic, and hostage negotiations. You can see that much of this book has been informed by all types of negotiations—and in turn is applicable to these different realms.

The Physical Arrangements

The facilities where any negotiation is to take place can be very important. If you are not in control of the facilities, be aware that they may be manipulated to the advantage of the other party. On the other hand, experienced negotiators know that the other party will be much more likely to agree to a proposal if they feel relaxed in the comfort zone of their home territory. If you travel to the other party's office, they are more likely to feel comfortable and receptive to your negotiation proposal. Furthermore, if at any time they need to consult with their staff or specialist advisors or if they need access to information or other resources during the negotiation, then they can do this more easily at their own base. One final advantage may be that if you need to use the high-risk close of an ultimatum, then you can always walk out of their office; this is a ploy that is much more difficult if you are in your office and they are the guests.

If you can control the arrangements, consider what tone you want to set. Choose the location and the room carefully and make sure it is laid out the way you want well before the start time. If the negotiation needs to remain secret, the location may need to be secure. Check that the routes to the location and to the room are appropriate and give the impression you want to create.

Check that the type of flooring suits your purpose. Tiled or wooden spaces may generate echoes when people speak. Carpets and soft furnishings can absorb or soften sounds. Consider if you need to use microphones, and test all such aids before the start. If you are in a very hot or very cold climate, you will want to decide how to adjust the internal temperature and humidity. In some locations that may be as simple as opening or closing the windows!

Lighting can make a big difference, so decide whether natural daylight is required or whether subdued lighting is better for the mood you want to create. Consider whether window blinds are needed, particularly so that nobody is sitting against light so bright that it is difficult for other people to see their expressions. Lighting from various angles will reduce the effects of shadows. Spotlights may be useful for working tables, while uplighters and shades may be better if you want diffuse light for the main space. Tungsten filaments give a warm glow, but you may prefer the cool look of fluorescent lights. Other types of filaments may be important, for example, if you are a sales organization intending to display products where colors are critical.

When there are several people to be seated around a table, they will need space so that any electronic devices they can use, or papers or notes they make, all remain confidential. Consider if you want to provide a space with video or audio-conferencing facilities, Internet access, a whiteboard, a projector, or just a flipchart where ideas can be sketched and discussed. You may want to provide a separate space where people can sit or stand taking refreshments and having informal chats.

Typically, conference facilities will have tables in the center, with chairs around the sides. Consider if you want to create the impression of a chairperson at one end or if a round table may be better. Tables can be perceived as barriers between negotiators, but some people feel more comfortable with a table in front of them, preferably with a vanity panel to hide feet and legs, which otherwise could disclose body language signals. If you are negotiating with two or more people, try to sit where you can watch them all so that you can be easily aware of their body language.

If there are just two people in your team, you have to decide whether you want to sit together so that you can quietly and quickly confer or sit apart so you can more easily be perceived as two distinct personalities. Some schools of thought say that if you are in a larger team than the other party, you should sit your team together, as a display of power. However, there are oftentimes when you will want to tone down that sort of impression to relax the other party and encourage them toward a "win-win" resolution. Conversely, some negotiators prefer to interlace their small team with the other party's larger team in an attempt to diffuse their apparent power.

Some negotiators feel that sitting directly across a table from one another creates a confrontational setting that could be avoided by a more informal arrangement that allows people to be at a slight angle to one another so they are not directly face to face but can easily maintain eye contact when appropriate. You could consider having just chairs, perhaps with small side tables on which to put things without hiding any body language. Decide what type of seating will help create the mood you intend: sofas to remove barriers, armchairs that allow participants to sit back, or upright chairs that tend to keep people leaning forward. Sometimes the problem with soft sofas is that people tend to slump and lean back, which may give the impression that they are not really focused and interested. Upright chairs will support people in a posture that may be more indicative of attention and active listening. Check that there are no obvious large differences in the height of seats so you can be sure nobody feels unusually high or low in comparison to the others.

In short, pay appropriate attention to the physical arrangements so that, as a minimum, they do not detract from your plan for the substance of the negotiation.

Strategic Framework for Negotiation

In working with our clients around the world we have found that ineffective negotiation is often due to the lack of an adequate framework to plan, guide, and support successful negotiations. Our commercial clients range from large international companies where you might expect there to be an effective support framework to small enterprises where you may not be surprised to find no adequate internal advice or processes to allow negotiations to be more successful. Most of these organizations know they must maintain an effective business strategy; they recognize the importance of creating a relevant purchasing strategy and put a lot of thought into their sales strategy. However, many do not seem to realize that it is equally vital to develop a negotiation strategy for the whole organization. We often see organizations drift into negotiations without being properly prepared because they failed to recognize that the process of buying or selling had flipped into the process of negotiation.

The type of organization that is most successful at managing the transition into negotiation is often the sort that buys its raw materials or inventories on a continuous basis. Many of its transactions only demand buying skills, but some will involve conflict that has to be resolved using negotiation skills. These organizations therefore become experienced in managing the transition from buying mode into negotiation mode. But that experience is often concentrated in a buying function dedicated to a production department and is not easily available to other internal functions, such as to information technology, whenever they need to make a major capital investment that may occur only once every few years. The IT function often drifts from buying mode into negotiation mode because the organization as a whole fails to pool the negotiation experience it has at its disposal.

Many sales functions are very professional, with sales objectives, strategies, plans, standards, processes, training, and support, yet they sometimes let opportunities slip through their fingers because they fail to recognize when the process of selling needs to be flipped into the process of negotiation. Even when individual salespeople spot the need to switch into their negotiation mode, the sales organization can often fail to support them, especially when they get close to the end of their accounting periods. There are often real worries at month end, escalating to anxieties at quarter end and culminating in an end of year panic. If the targets are in danger, there is a temptation to focus exclusively on tactics such as discounting to try to hit the target volumes. At these times, the support framework for negotiation can easily be pushed lower down the management priority list. Management may issue instructions that negotiations already in progress during the end of period panic should be closed right away, even if the salespeople haven't yet reached the target positions they feel are very realistic. The danger is that end-of-period discounting can set the minimum expectation on prices for any repeat business from that customer and all the other potential customers who have relevant contacts and good market intelligence. The other party will learn very quickly to hold out until the end of period panic sets in. Future negotiations may be in danger of being sabotaged by the actions of senior sales executives.

Some sales functions develop good negotiation strategies and a framework of processes and support for their salespeople, but this good practice can be rather localized and does not benefit the organization as a whole. This is particularly visible to us in some large international companies with diverse regional sales divisions. Decentralization often delivers excellent flexibility and responsiveness to customers and opportunities but makes it more of a challenge for top management to ensure that successful ideas about negotiation from one sales division can be promulgated to others.

In our experience, what is needed by many organizations is better balanced top management support for their negotiation framework. A good start is to ensure that a single vice president or director is empowered and held accountable for all aspects of the negotiation strategy and framework across all the management silos in the organization. That does not necessarily imply a change to the organizational structure, but it does call for a matrix management approach with one person owning the "horizontal" process for negotiation no matter which "vertical" organizational structures it crosses and no matter which regions are involved. That vice president should ensure there are senior managers in both sales and purchasing empowered and accountable for the lower-level processes that support and enable negotiations. They should also be held accountable for the recruitment, induction, development, and training of individuals with the right balance of skills.

Management information is, of course, critical in all organizations regardless of their size, but we often find it is lacking on the subject of negotiation. However, those organizations that consistently outperform others in negotiation usually have a system of quantifying, recording, and analyzing their performance and monitoring statistical trends. This helps them to make improvements in their negotiation processes and to pinpoint where additional training may be required. Summarized management information about overall performance in negotiations should be presented to the upper levels of executive management. Relevant data should be available on the "executive dashboard" so that top management can monitor and evaluate how well their negotiation strategy and processes are working.

Reflective Practice and Coaching in Negotiation

Our experience is that all sizes and types of organizations can benefit from some simple steps to help them capitalize on their own negotiation experience and to draw on other advice and resources. One technique is called *reflective practice*. This is used in many different professions. In this context, it is the process of considering in a structured manner the outcomes from each negotiation, comparing them to the expected outcomes and then discussing how improvements can be made to the way future negotiations are managed. Reflective practice can help people identify where they made a mistake in their last negotiation and then decide what they can strive to do differently in their next one. In a small enterprise, this may be as simple as the one and only negotiator working through a checklist to try to evaluate what went well and what could be improved for the next time. In larger organizations with several people involved in their own negotiations and perhaps with teams of negotiators, the reflective practice can benefit from both individual and group input. Each negotiator must take accountability for their own reflective practice, but this can be much more effective when supplemented by regular coaching from mentors.

Negotiators and their mentors or coaches need to be able to work well together. There needs to be good personal relationships built on trust and respect. Some senior managers may be effective negotiators but lack the ability or the time to support and encourage other people. Some negotiators may be reluctant to be open about their own perceived weaknesses, particularly if the mentor is also the person responsible for performance evaluation and pay! To avoid these problems, it can be useful to have an internal center of expertise and advice, where people can share their experiences, reflect on their own skills, and exchange ideas on how performance can be improved by the individual and by better processes within the organization. We have found that for some businesses, an informal system of "peer group" support and advice can be more effective than direct line-management initiatives. In larger organizations, the center of expertise and support can be extended to help people prepare plans for upcoming negotiations. It can also be a good source of advice during a lengthy negotiation when it is possible to break off and "phone a friend." The other extreme may be found in a competitive internal environment, where your peer may be a colleague who you are in competition with and maybe don't particularly like. Often, receiving that person's acidic criticism of your negotiation skills can be much more enlightening than accepting watered-down advice from a friend who may not want to be overly critical.

A Common Vocabulary

In small enterprises, there is usually little difficulty in communicating issues on the subject of negotiation. However, as organizations grow and particularly when they have a presence in diverse parts of the world, it often gets more difficult for negotiators to share experiences and learn from each other. Many of our clients benefit from establishing a single framework of negotiation concepts using a common vocabulary and shared processes. The investment of effort quickly pays for itself because improvements can be promulgated rapidly throughout the organization. Individuals find it easier to discuss their performance and agree on what they can do better next time. The organization as a whole finds it easier to analyze trends and discuss "hot spots" that would benefit from corrective action to processes.

Such a framework of negotiation concepts, using a common vocabulary, can best be established through a companywide program of negotiation training. This also enables effective, ongoing coaching by allowing negotiators to pinpoint a small number of techniques that they want to improve or new practices that they need to adopt in the immediate future. The mentor system enables an effective discussion of these learning targets and a more formal and overt commitment to achieve the desired improvements. The individuals can practice these techniques in a nonthreatening environment and then try them in live negotiations. Once they feel confident about that small set of improvements, they can identify a further small number of techniques to try in the following period. Their mentor or peer group will help to quantify learning targets and to measure progress.

The Virtual Coach

For organizations that are unable to maintain a dedicated center of expertise because of their small size or geographical diversity, they may be able to
identify external resources to help. RDC offers a full training and support
service, including an option for online access. This provides a framework of
negotiation concepts using a common vocabulary and training materials in the
form of online access to DVDs and books. This can be extended to personal
coaching to give expert advice to negotiators facing consistent problems or
challenges and for mentoring in advanced negotiation techniques. RDC also
provides consultancy services to organizations that need to develop their
negotiation strategy and their framework to plan, guide, and support successful negotiations.

Summary and Conclusion

We've gone through some key points that will help you enhance your negotiation skills. We've defined negotiation and looked at the alternative strategies for conflict resolution. We have explored the philosophical points that allow you to create your own personal mantras for engagement in "win-win" negotiation. You are now familiar with the five phases of every negotiation, and you have the ten golden rules providing guidance for your next deal. We've emphasized the critical importance of planning and gone through the RDC ten-point plan, and out of this we've expanded on the jellyfish analogy so you can make flexible and intelligent proposals. You now know about the "negotiation bow tie" that can help you to create additional value above and beyond the value that either of the parties involved in the negotiation could find in isolation—what has been called a "super-win." You are also aware of the key cross-cultural issues in negotiation. We have discussed some similarities and differences between commercial, hostage, and diplomatic negotiations, and we've identified the lessons that each can learn from the others. We have explored various ways in which a deadlock can be broken. You also have some ideas to consider around the physical arrangements and facilities for a negotiation. For organizations, we have stressed the need to develop a negotiation strategy and a framework to plan, guide, and support successful negotiations. Finally, you have seen the importance of reflective practice, coaching, and support in negotiation.

To be a great negotiator is to have discipline, creativity, and courage. You can now use the content of this book to build your confidence and to be there as reference material when you are planning your next negotiation. Be assured that if you apply this wealth of material, you will become a great negotiator.

Many of our clients have been businesses that have learned how to sell more successfully. Other clients have improved their buying skills. A few clients have applied our techniques outside the business environment altogether—in such areas as international diplomatic services. We are confident that you too will benefit from this book. Thanks for reading it. We are sure you will find this of practical use throughout your career, and we leave you with our very best wishes for your continuing success.

Negotiating Styles

Table A-1 summarizes the three negotiating styles covered in *Getting to Yes: Negotiating Agreement Without Giving In* by Roger Fisher, William L. Ury, and Bruce Patton (Penguin Books, 1991).

Table A-1. Summary of Three Negotiating Styles

Soft	Hard	Principled
Participants are friends.	Participants are adversaries.	Participants are problem-solvers.
The goal is agreement.	The goal is victory.	The goal is a wise outcome reached efficiently and amicably.
Make concessions to cultivate the relationship.	Demand concessions as a condition of the relationship.	Separate the people from the problem.
Be soft on the people and the problem.	Be hard on the problem and the people.	Be soft on the people but hard on the problem.
Trust others.	Distrust others.	Proceed independent of trust.
Change your position easily.	Dig into your position.	Focus on interests, not on positions.
Make offers.	Make threats.	Explore interests.

(continued)

Table A-1. (*continued*)

Soft	Hard	Principled
Disclose your bottom line.	Mislead as to your bottom line.	Avoid having a bottom line.
Accept one-sided losses to reach agreement.	Demand one-sided gains as the price of agreement.	Invent options for mutual gain.
Search for the single answer (the one they will accept).	Search for the single answer (the one you will accept).	Develop multiple options to choose from (decide later).
Insist on agreement.	Insist on your position.	Insist on using objective criteria.
Try to avoid a contest of will.	Try to win a contest of will.	Try to reach a result based on standards independent of will.
Yield to pressure.	Apply pressure.	Reason and be open to reason; yield to principle, not to pressure.

Negotiation Influence Behaviors

Table B-1 summarizes and paraphrases the ten categories of influence behavior, based on the 2002 article "Influencing in Hostage Negotiations: The Table of Ten" by Ellen Giebels.

Table B-1. Ten Categories of Influence Behavior

Strategy	Underlying Principle	Description of Behavior
Being kind	Sympathy	Exhibiting friendly, helpful behavior
Being equal	Similarity	Using statements aimed at something the parties have in common
Being credible	Authority	Showing expertise or proving you are reliable
Emotional appeal	Self-image	Playing upon the emotions of the other party
Intimidation	Deterrence/fear	Threatening with punishment or accusing the other personally
Imposing a restriction	Scarcity	Delaying behavior or making something available in a limited way

(continued)

Table B-1. (*continued*)

Strategy	Underlying Principle	Description of Behavior
Direct pressure	Power of repetition	Exerting pressure on the other in a neutral manner by being firm
Legitimizing	Legitimacy	Referring to what has been agreed upon in society or with the other party
Exchanging	Reciprocity	Engaging in give-and-take behaviors
Rational persuasion	Consistency	Using persuasive arguments and logic

Index

I

Get the eBook for only $10!

This Apress title will prove so indispensible that you'll want to carry it with you everywhere, which is why we are offering the eBook in 3 formats for only $10 if you have already purchased the print book.

Convenient and fully searchable, the PDF version enables you to easily find and copy code—or perform examples by quickly toggling between instructions and applications. The MOBI format is ideal for your Kindle, while the ePUB can be utilized on a variety of mobile devices.

Go to www.apress.com/promo/tendollars to purchase your companion eBook.

Apress®
THE EXPERT'S VOICE™

Other Apress Business Titles You Will Find Useful

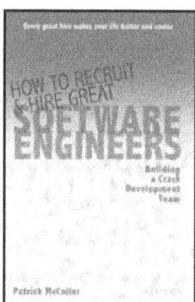

Available at www.apress.com

Ingram Content Group UK Ltd.
Milton Keynes UK
UKHW041304210523
422093UK00001B/90

9 781484 208519